Praise

THE SOUL-SOAR
OF SEPARATION

'What a beautifully simple but profound book – where was it
when I needed it! It's like a scroll through Instagram that leaves
you feeling hopeful and strong. Each part of it will help every
woman who reads it, especially if they are going through the
painful process that surrounds the ending of a relationship or
marriage. It's one to keep in your bag, by your bedside, and turn
to when you need that little reminder that it will all be okay.'

ANDREA MCLEAN, #1 *SUNDAY TIMES* BESTSELLING AUTHOR, BROADCASTER AND
CO-FOUNDER OF FEMALE EMPOWERMENT SITE WWW.THISGIRLISONFIRE.COM

'This is a breathtaking book – deeply galvanizing and empowering. Amy
expertly provides real, practical and relatable wisdom in such an easily
digestible way. You will feel wrapped up in a warm embrace, like you are
being softly guided through the challenge of loss and grief into glorious
rebirth. This book will help you find your truth, your clarity and the
energy to see you through to a fresh new purposeful chapter of life.'

SUZY READING, PSYCHOLOGIST AND AUTHOR OF *SELF-CARE FOR TOUGH TIMES*

'Powerful and moving. This is a very special book.'

ZOE BLASKEY, FOUNDER OF MOTHERKIND

'Amy's book shines a light on all the ways that we can
embrace a challenging situation like separation as a huge
opportunity for growth and positive new beginnings.'

ZOË DESMOND, FOUNDER OF FROLO, THE SINGLE PARENT COMMUNITY APP

THE SOUL-SOARING VIRTUES OF SEPARATION

THE SOUL-SOARING VIRTUES OF SEPARATION

111 learnings to heal your heart
and help you fly

AMY RANSOM

HAY HOUSE

Carlsbad, California • New York City
London • Sydney • New Delhi

Published in the United Kingdom by:
Hay House UK Ltd, The Sixth Floor, Watson House,
54 Baker Street, London W1U 7BU
Tel: +44 (0)20 3927 7290; Fax: +44 (0)20 3927 7291; www.hayhouse.co.uk

Published in the United States of America by:
Hay House Inc., PO Box 5100, Carlsbad, CA 92018-5100
Tel: (1) 760 431 7695 or (800) 654 5126
Fax: (1) 760 431 6948 or (800) 650 5115; www.hayhouse.com

Published in Australia by:
Hay House Australia Ltd, 18/36 Ralph St, Alexandria NSW 2015
Tel: (61) 2 9669 4299; Fax: (61) 2 9669 4144; www.hayhouse.com.au

Published in India by:
Hay House Publishers India, Muskaan Complex,
Plot No.3, B-2, Vasant Kunj, New Delhi 110 070
Tel: (91) 11 4176 1620; Fax: (91) 11 4176 1630; www.hayhouse.co.in

A catalogue record for this book is available from the British Library.

Tradepaper ISBN: 978-1-78817-514-2
E-book ISBN: 978-1-78817-547-0
Audiobook ISBN: 978-1-78817-595-1

Interior images: v, 1, 41, 73, 99, 141, 167, 199, 235 Shutterstock.com/Natalia Alexeeva; xv, xvii, 3, 43, 75, 101, 143, 169, 201, 237, 293, 295 Shutterstock. com/ksanask.art-studio; all other images Shutterstock.com/krisArt

Printed and bound by CPI Group (UK) Ltd, Croydon, CR0 4YY

To Donna and Claudia, for soaring.
And to Sarah, for helping me fly.

CONTENTS

≫ PART 2: MOTIVATION ≪

≫ PART 3: INSIGHT ≪

>>> PART 4: SELF-EXPRESSION <<<

❧ PART 5: UNIQUENESS ☙

❧ PART 6: INDEPENDENCE ☙

Contents

≫➤ PART 7: AWAKENING ◄≪

≫➤ PART 8: NEW BEGINNINGS ◄≪

TO YOU,
MY LOVELY READER

I never imagined I would write about separation, following my own in 2016 at the age of 39, after nine years of marriage, three children and 14 years of being together. It's such a personal experience.

Then one day, during my daily run, I was listening to Oprah's Super Soul podcast with Sarah Ban Breathnach, author of *The New York Times* bestseller, *Simple Abundance*. She shared how she wrote the book for *her*, never once thinking about the effect it might have on others.

Right there and then, I knew I wanted to write *this* book. Not to dwell on what went 'wrong', blame, mourn or overshare, but to put into words what *I've* been shown about myself during this time.

Because for me, separation – while occasionally challenging and painful – has been my greatest opportunity yet to really and truly get to know myself. I believe it can be one of the most positive experiences in life and the gateway to fulfilling our true potential. If we choose and allow it to be so.

Separation, in its many forms, is a heady mix of conflicting emotions, often hitting all at once. But I know that *you* can fly. That you will learn to accept these emotions *and* learn from them. And that, some days, your soul will soar higher than ever before.

This I have been shown, over and over again.

THE STORY BEHIND THIS
BOOK AND HOW TO USE IT

*'You have the ability to quickly change your patterns of thought,
and eventually your life experience.'*

ABRAHAM HICKS

Shortly after I separated, I was introduced to the concept of the Law of Attraction: the theory that we draw everything ('manifest' them) into our lives with our thoughts, energy and vibration (the energy we emit). We attract the positive. Likewise, we attract the negative. The ultimate state of being is to be in alignment with ourselves – an energetic match for whatever it is that we desire. We have to feel like the person we want to be without actually being it (yet).

The timing of my discovery seemed to me to be pure chance. In time, I was to learn that it was no coincidence. Nothing ever is.

I grasped very swiftly that I alone could influence my circumstances. It wasn't about changing them, it was about changing *myself* within them and going on to attract positive circumstances, which I actually wanted.

In the realm of separation, this approach changed *everything* for me because it took separation from being an undesirable state to an empowering one. It took me from being 'victim' to victorious.

The Law of Attraction is the main philosophy behind this book, together with the ideas of so many amazing authors and thought-leaders who have enlightened my life through their books and podcasts, which have 'appeared' when I needed them most. I hope I have interpreted them faithfully.

Once the urge came to write this book, I saw that I had a lot to say about separation. I wanted it to be easy to read and reference; when your head is in a fog and you're emotionally drained or stuck, it's so important that any salvation you're offered is easily accessible. This book is split into eight parts and 111 learnings. The '111' was instinctive and deliberate on my part because, in the field of numerology, 111 is one of the most powerful numbers. It carries the combined attributes of 1 – associated with independence, uniqueness, new beginnings, insight and self-leadership – and the master number 11, which represents awakening, enlightenment and learning to understand our soul mission and life purpose. These very powerful stages form the sections of the book.

Every one of them is present in separation.

The learnings are mine but this book is for you, also: whether you've picked it up in a place of limbo on the brink of separation; you've just separated; you're divorced and struggling to move forwards; you have kids or not; or you're experiencing first heartbreak after losing the love of your life.

This book is not intended to be a guide to the practical aspects of separation – everyone's circumstances are so different – but rather to enable you to handle *whatever* circumstances you find yourself navigating. It's less about 'telling' you what to do and more about helping you to 'feel' your way. We are all unique in our motivation and actions: what lifts me from the fog won't necessarily lift you. But I believe there is much common ground in how we wish to feel and this book is about helping you to identify what that means for you.

When I write 'I' or 'me', I hope you'll picture *yourself*. Read the book in one go, or dip in and out of it as you choose whenever you need some encouragement to keep going or a reminder of how far you've come. Use it as a daily affirmation tool to focus your energy by flicking the pages randomly and seeing which one you land on. The universe will always make sure you land on the page you need in that moment. It might also help you to know that I still read, revisit and remind myself of my own learnings here: it's a continual journey, if we're moving and growing as we should be.

And it doesn't matter if souls and universes aren't your language. You don't have to be a spiritual leader, expert, or devote yourself to three months of silence to be able to benefit from *really* getting to know yourself and trust in your soul. I am an ordinary mum of three; I haven't 'heard' silence since 2009 but I am handed all the experiences I need, every day, to keep growing and learning to be more stable in my vibration.

Most importantly of all, begin to put yourself first. Be nice to *you*. Cultivate positive thoughts. And avoid speaking words not rooted in love, especially about your ex-partner; such words don't nurture your spirit or illuminate your path.

Create a present and future you want to live.

Become victorious.

PART 1

ASSERTIVENESS

APPROACHING SEPARATION IN THE BEGINNING

S eparation is unsettling.

The beginning of separation presents us with a choice. How do we want to approach it? Because, if there is no going back, then there is only going forwards.

We can choose to do this assertively, even on the days we feel really, really sad. I believe it makes a difference when we get to say how we want it to be. What we want our own separation to look like. It can then be an empowering position to find ourselves in, not a pitiful one.

We only have to choose it to be so.

The 14 learnings in this first part are all about that.

Learning 1
I WILL KNOW WHEN
THE TIME IS RIGHT

'Whatever I need to know is revealed to me
in the perfect time–space sequence.'
LOUISE HAY, *TRUST LIFE*

People often ask me, 'How did you know?' or 'When did you decide to separate?' The truth is, I didn't know and I didn't decide, until it actually happened.

I think it's probably rare to plan a separation like you do a wedding – 'Today's the day! Save the date!' However you separate, it's my experience from talking to others that there comes a time when someone says, 'Enough.' Or, possibly, someone just leaves.

For me, at least, this is what happened. The situation escalated until I could ignore it no longer. And, although the end of my marriage had been looming for a long time, although, in retrospect, I see that I had actually made myself a loose promise that I would leave if it didn't get any better by the time our son was two, I still didn't know that 4 August 2016 was to be the last day of my marriage or that my ex-husband would never sleep in our house again. Until it came.

In fact, I was in a good mood that day. I had spent it in the park with my three kids and some friends. I was thinking about getting a bottle of wine for dinner. After some very frank conversations earlier that year and a discussion about separating, I had really been trying to make our marriage work. Then, on my ex-husband's way home from work, he sent me a text message. In that one text, I found the clarity that I'd been searching for all year.

I suddenly saw that *everything* in our marriage had broken down, from what I perceived to be his lack of respect for me to our non-existent communication. There was nothing left to save. By what I would eventually learn was absolutely no coincidence, our son had turned two only a month earlier.

It was the only way our marriage *could* end. Strongly and quickly. That was how it was to be, for us. Every time prior to that day we just hadn't been ready, or desperate enough, to say goodbye.

So I no longer believe in forcing time or decisions, in any area of my life, even when I feel that something isn't quite right. Sometimes, it takes a process and other experiences to allow us to end up where we are always meant to be. And all we have to do during that time is *allow* those experiences to happen. Remember, we are always moving in the direction of our *own* purpose (see Learning 97).

If you're in an unhappy relationship and not sure *how* to end it, give yourself time to get there and trust that, if separation is truly what you want and what is best for you, you will know when the time is right. Just as I did.

If you've been left heartbroken and had the decision of separation taken away from you – I am so sorry for what you're going through. I hope that the learnings that follow will allow you to regain a sense of self and empowerment, while naturally grieving the loss of your partner and your relationship (which we *all* do, by the way, regardless of who left whom). I also hope it helps you when I say I *truly* believe that the situation you've found yourself in gives you an even greater chance to soar and discover who you really are.

Learning 2

I WILL UNDERSTAND
HOW I GOT HERE

'Life is basically unfair. But even in a situation that's unfair,
I think it's possible to seek out a kind of fairness.'
HARUKI MURAKAMI, *WHAT I TALK ABOUT WHEN I TALK ABOUT RUNNING*

There are two sides to every story.

But it requires an honest and open person to be able to see those two sides when you're the protagonist, not an objective narrator.

I didn't *blame* my ex-husband for our separation but I did think it was his fault. I am totally aware of the irony of this statement. I thought it was the 'flaws' in his character and *his* behaviour that had got us to this point.

It took a very wise friend, in tune with the universe, to point out that, in fact, it was me who had sealed the end of my marriage the day I silently aired *that* promise to leave, after our third and final baby was born.

I could have thrown a different thought out into the universe – *I will stay in this marriage and choose to love and accept my husband* – but instead, I had already chosen to leave.

This insight started the very important process of self-reflection for me. A process of taking responsibility for *my* role in our separation and acknowledging the most important fact of all; I hadn't loved him enough. Our foundations were rocky from the very beginning yet foolishly we had still tried to build a house.

Certainly, he wasn't blameless in our marriage or its demise. But, then again, neither was I. After all, ultimately, I chose to marry him. And then to separate from him. I was mostly an active participant in all that happened in between, not a passive one.

Why did this help me when it didn't change the outcome? Because it allowed me to move from a place of feeling like a victim or, even worse, a martyr to a place of responsibility, where I could see that actually I had steered my own ship and the universe had handed me *exactly* what I'd asked for. It allowed me to move forwards, assertively, in my life as a single woman and mother. With power, not pity.

While your story will be different to mine and your arrival here will be too, doing a little self-reflection to see how and where you are accountable as a result of the decisions you've made up until this point will liberate you. From some anger and blame, at the very least. Try it.

And take the time to understand how *you* got here.

Learning 3
I HAVE
A CHOICE, NOW

*'You may not control all the events that happen to you,
but you can decide not to be reduced by them.'*
MAYA ANGELOU, *LETTER TO MY DAUGHTER*

Relationships break down. Because this book is all about going forwards, we won't look at the myriad reasons they end. Some are a shock and end suddenly. Others are more gradual and, perhaps, even inevitable. In between there are a thousand other scenarios too.

Ultimately, we find ourselves in the same place. On our own. Without the person who was once standing by our side.

What do you do next? How do you go on? Especially if you didn't choose it? How do you possibly make sense of it all?

Start with this: 'I have a choice, *now*.'

Because you do have a choice and the choice you make *now* is your new foundation, for all that follows. Why not make it a strong and positive one?

I talked to myself gently and avoided defining my experience with 'effort' words such as 'tough' and 'fight'. I didn't want to *fight*. And, for me, it was when I chose to frame my separation and new status as a position of empowerment, not as a tragedy or a desperate statistic, that things changed significantly and rapidly.

The more empowered I felt, the more empowerment I attracted. I now know that this is how it works – you invite in more of whatever you're giving out.

Since that day, I have been able to see that I own *every* decision I make and *every* thought I create, whether it turns out as I'd hoped or not. I try hard not to be a victim or martyr (I don't always succeed, of course).

If you're reading this and the end of your relationship wasn't your choice, this possibly feels like a tall order. Maybe even an impossible one.

But, just so you know it *is* possible, however it happens, let me briefly tell you about an incredible friend who was left by her husband under the most challenging of circumstances, while she was pregnant and with two small children already. I watched her in awe as she made the choice to move on and own what came next, not without its painful moments of course, but with determination, nonetheless. I'm not sure I've ever believed in the strength of our own personal spirit so much, or in how we can turn a situation around *ourselves*, until I had the honour of standing by her side.

But now I believe in the spirit's absoluteness. And, trust me, yours is no exception. You have a choice now, too.

Learning 4

I CAN INFLUENCE HOW
PEOPLE REACT

'Example is not the main thing in influencing
others. It is the only thing.'
ALBERT SCHWEITZER, *UNITED NATIONS WORLD* MAGAZINE

You'll possibly discover that when people find out about the end of your relationship, you'll be inundated with words of sorrow.

The end of a relationship is one of the worst things that many can imagine happening. Being alone is undesirable and catastrophic; that's what those people seem to believe. But they don't know the liberation, empowerment and pure joy of starting a new relationship that will come to be the most important one of your life. The relationship you have with *yourself*.

They might never get an opportunity to know this.

Of course, if separation wasn't your choice, initially you're likely to want to hear some sympathetic words – at least from those closest to you. But, once you're feeling more in alignment with the reality of separation and more peaceful, why would you choose to be the subject of someone else's pity, especially when you're not feeling the sorrow so intensely any more?

It's far more bolstering to hear positive and encouraging words from others, words that mirror the position of strength we're starting to find ourselves in, ever so gradually. It helps us firm up that belief that we *can* move on, that this is *not* a catastrophe. It gives us permission, when we're vulnerable and we need it.

I have found that I can always influence how people react to anything I tell them; by my facial expressions, my tone, my body language and what's going on in my eyes. It's more *how* I say it than *what* I say.

When I told people, I simply said, 'We've separated. But it's honestly fine. It was coming for a long time and we're all doing really well.' I always smiled.

In those three sentences, I left no room for someone to question me further, or to feel sorry for me. It was really important for me to own that conversation; to normalize it and remove any sense of tragedy from it.

You can also use the same approach when telling any children you may have. Being confident in your delivery – even if you aren't completely feeling it yet and there are still many things to iron out – will give your kids an initial foundation of strength and reassure them that this is not a huge tragedy that is going to ruin their lives forever. It's also okay, by the way, if the announcement of your separation does *not* start this way; my children witnessed our relationship deteriorate over a year or so and culminate in a rather intense argument. But I did find the right moment afterwards to inject some positivity and confidence into them and help them start to believe that this *would* make their lives better.

Relationships break up. But that is *never* the end.

It's the wonder of a new beginning. That not everyone gets to *know*.

If you're not there yet, don't worry, you'll see soon enough.

Learning 5
I AM
BREATHING AGAIN

'Practise moderation in all things except love.'
GARY ZUKAV

For a long time, my marriage suffocated me. I had been running out of breath until, one day, I couldn't breathe at all.

While there were many good things in my life, the love and respect of a partner was not one of them. Despite telling myself over and over again that I could exist without this, because I had so much love elsewhere, the truth became glaringly obvious; I couldn't.

The physical absence of having a partner and the longing for love and companionship is one thing, as I have since learned. But the absence of love when you actually *have* someone somehow feels much lonelier. It stifles that hope we have when we are single – that excitement at the possibility of finding love and making a real connection with another person.

That absence bore down on me like an enormous, crushing weight. I see now that it stopped me from fulfilling the potential of my true, open and loving self. Because deep down I was unhappy and low on self-esteem, and neither of those do anything to nurture the growth of love for yourself.

The moment my marriage ended, that weight instantly lifted. 'You look lighter,' said one of the few friends who knew, a few weeks later. 'Your face, your shoulders, everything.'

I *felt* lighter. Because a decision had been made. Finally. I had reached an outcome and there was no more living in limbo, denial or an unsatisfactory acceptance of love in moderation.

It was, of course, only the start of my journey. I knew that I had a huge trek ahead of me and I didn't *really* know how to begin it, aside from putting one foot in front of the other and taking one day at a time, which is what I continue to do.

What I did come to know is that my desire for love, whether that was loving another or developing the ability to express *self*-love, was as great as my need for oxygen – if not greater.

When you acknowledge that your relationship may be starving you of air, suddenly you can start to breathe again.

Learning 6
I TAKE
ONE DAY AT A TIME

*'I'm beginning to recognize that real happiness isn't
something large...but something small, numerous
and already here. The smile of someone you love.
A decent breakfast. The warm sunset.'*

BEAU TAPLIN, *BURIED LIGHT*

Those first few days and weeks of separation were really strange and contradictory.

On one hand, I just wanted to fast-forward to a time when it would all feel better, where it would all feel 'right' and 'normal' (before I knew the illusion behind such words). On the other hand, I felt empowered, almost invincible. The moment my marriage ended, my energy changed and the good things kept happening. It felt like one amazing thing after another. My self-published book took off. I turned 40. I approached an agent and got a book deal, while raising three kids, mostly on my own.

I didn't realize what a high I had been on until I crashed, 14 months later, and just collapsed on the bottom step of my stairs and cried. Really cried. I felt *all* the sadness and 'tragedy' of my separation in that one moment. I think it was the first time I had cried much, at all.

Immediately I felt calmer, and I listened to that moment and what it wanted to tell me: 'Slow down. Process. Be more still. You do not need to fix everything or strive continually.' So I allowed myself to feel sad, on *that* particular day. Because it's what I needed to do. Just be sad. The next day, I didn't feel quite so hopeless.

And I have since learned that this is what separation looks like. There will never be a time where it all feels 'right'. I accept that there doesn't need to be; so I've stopped looking. Life is always changing. And so are we. This change happens when we're married or in a relationship, so it makes perfect sense that it also happens in separation. Yet I think we expect it to be otherwise. We see separation as a problem to be fixed. To be resolved. Only then can we move on with making our life 'right' again. Perfect, even.

But we never need to wait for such a grand conclusion. We can start today and be happy, in some form, *today*. Taking one day at a time is magical (even when the day, itself, is not). Because a day in isolation is a glorious thing. It becomes precious, not just one amidst 365 of them.

Notice *today* – really look at it – and you'll see that there is *always* some good to be found. Even if, right now, the *only* good you can find is a good cup of coffee or the fact that tomorrow holds the promise of feeling a little bit better. More peaceful.

Each new day is a stepping stone away from suffering in the direction of your new future. What will it hold? Where will it take you? Who will it bring you? The uncertainty of this is quite thrilling, when we allow it to be.

Why not take hold of the empowering days, full of loving and creative energy, when they happen? Feel invincible. Grateful. *Possible*. By contrast, when there are days where you have to try *really* hard not to feel like a victim, assertively remind yourself of the choices that may have got you here. Take back your power.

Because you are not a victim and neither am I; we are people who can do *anything* with every magical day that lies ahead of us.

Learning 7
I ACCEPT ALL OF MY EMOTIONS

*'Instead of resisting any emotion, the best
way to dispel it is to enter it fully, embrace
it and see through your resistance.'*

DEEPAK CHOPRA

Nothing brings out such a conflict of emotions as loss. Separation is a form of loss and all of us who find ourselves here must grieve that loss.

We have to let go of an ideal of a life we had been living. A future we were pursuing. And, now, we are being forced to recognize uncertainty, which, while being one of the greatest gifts separation gives us (more on this later), can initially make us feel really uncomfortable and lost.

Here are three things I have learned about emotions:

~   I am not my emotions.

~   I do not need to resist my emotions.

~   My emotions will pass.

No one likes to get angry, resentful or so consumed by sadness that they feel they are losing all sense of their rational self. When it happens to me, afterwards I feel more anger *towards* the anger. I certainly feel disappointed in myself because I perceive I've let myself down reacting like that. Sound familiar? We associate ourselves too strongly with our emotions, whatever they are in that moment. But we *aren't* our emotions and it isn't helpful to see ourselves in this way. Because when we distance ourselves from how we are feeling and recognize the emotion we are feeling without judging it, we are more able to lean back from it and be an objective observer instead of an over-invested host.

Judging our emotions always triggers resistance, which takes us yet further out of alignment with ourselves. We tell ourselves we shouldn't be feeling this way, which causes more suffering. But if we simply observe the emotion without getting too involved with it, there is no resistance at all and we can simply allow ourselves to feel *however* we feel in that given moment. We stay in alignment with ourselves and the emotion eventually passes.

Every emotion you feel is still valid. And you are likely to feel many of them, often all at once. So, don't judge any of them. Accept the sadness you feel. When you feel angry, try and observe the anger. Where is it *really* coming from? Often, our anger is misdirected at someone else, when actually we have a niggle with *ourselves* that we just need to understand before showing ourselves some sympathy and compassion. There's more about emotional awareness in Learning 50.

For now, remember. You are not your emotions. You do not need to resist your emotions. Your emotions will pass.

I TAKE THE PHYSICAL SPACE I DESERVE

'Wisdom comes with the ability to be still.'
ECKHART TOLLE, *STILLNESS SPEAKS*

Every beginning is new to us, whether it's one we welcome or one we initially fear. Sometimes, new beginnings are a combination of both.

A new job. A new house. A new relationship status.

We haven't been there before. We don't know what it will feel like or how we will react.

So we must *lean back*, not rush in. I'll repeat this phrase a lot in this book because it is such an effective state, which I practise daily.

Sometimes, the only way to do this is to give ourselves the physical space we deserve. We must just allow ourselves to *be*, without trying to 'cure' ourselves or fill every moment with distractions or others.

We are never meant to be 'cured' or fixed. To be 'fixed' would be to erase all the things that have happened to us in our lives so far, and to give up learning more. We are meant to be *here*, in this situation, right now. It's our path and if we're too distracted or too busy to pay attention, we might miss where it's leading us.

The desire for certainty will be our obstacle here. We just want to *know* what's next. We crave that security and we are impatient to find it. From childhood, we have been taught that we must *make* things happen or we'll miss out. As an addictive 'doer', I have spent my whole life forcing. It's only since separation that I'm learning to recognize when I need to do less, even though that can occasionally still feel uncomfortable.

Have you ever found yourself rooted to the spot, unable to move? This happened to me after separation, the first time my children left the house to go to their dad's for the weekend. I sat on the floor in my bedroom for two hours and literally couldn't bring myself to get up – me, a usually energetic soul who likes to be busy. It was as if I was paralysed.

It still happens every now and again, except now I see it as a really essential part of my being. Because being quiet, still and giving ourselves some actual physical space, away from anyone else – basically the roots of meditation, without actually being aware we're meditating – is something this hectic world doesn't instinctively offer us amidst all the noise that constantly surrounds us.

When the noise is becoming too loud, I turn off my phone and cocoon myself at home. There is immediate calm in being available *only* to myself (and my children).

We are programmed to fear the state of being alone, to fear our own physical space.

And yet, it is in these quiet moments on our own that we gain the greatest clarity.

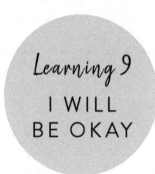

Learning 9
I WILL
BE OKAY

'If you believe it will work out, you'll see opportunities.
If you believe it won't, you will see obstacles."

WAYNE DYER

'I will be okay.'

We know this to be true. Deep within us. You might not feel it this very minute, but think of all the things you've withstood before that you didn't think you could. You were okay, weren't you?

It is, of course, incredibly easy to forget this and, sometimes, especially in the early days, and even beyond, we just need to remind ourselves, or be reassured by someone else, that we will be okay.

You will be okay.

In the moments where we are feeling far from it, where the sadness, uncertainty or anxiety makes us doubt this is our path, we can simply choose to trust in what comes next and not embrace the doubt.

Like everything in life, it is far easier to have faith when things are going well than when they are not. The true test is always how we stand when we feel like we're falling down.

And, my, is it a test some days.

My feelings in these moments tend to be resentment, blame and loneliness. I momentarily and conveniently choose to forget *how* I got here because it is less painful to put it all at the hands of another: my ex-husband; a friend who hasn't checked in; a family member who doesn't seem to appreciate just how stretched I am. None of these things bother me when I'm flying high, when I'm in the state of being that *knows* I don't need to rely on anyone but myself.

But when a day is hard, I want to be rescued. I revert to being a victim. When I am in this state of being, I can only perpetuate *this* state and its suffering. It has taken me a long time to learn that I must practise grace and gratitude and speak kind words to myself to lift me out. So, as I feel myself spiralling, I literally have to make a conscious choice to stop feeding the negativity and *say something nice*: about me; the person I was focusing my resentment on; or something I feel fortunate to have. Instantly, I can feel my energy change and it continues to build from there.

I also like to think that the tricky moments in separation have a positive purpose. They always propel me forwards and give me some further insight into myself. I see them as small bricks, which build me up and make me stand taller and stronger than before. A tower of resilience.

With time and practice, it gets easier to trust in the feeling of being okay – of all that we *know* to be true – because the more moments we successfully navigate, the more evidence we have to show us we will get through the next one. Fact.

In short, we can simply begin to trust that *being okay* is our ultimate truth.

And there is much reassurance and respite in accepting that.

I SHARE WHAT *I* CHOOSE
WITH *WHOM* I CHOOSE

'I don't know why people are so keen to put the details of their private life in public; they forget that invisibility is a superpower.'

BANKSY

Nothing garners interest like the breakdown of a relationship, especially if, as far as the outside world is concerned, it happened completely out of the blue.

Well, here's something to remember. You and *only* you choose when and with whom you wish to discuss it.

When my ex-husband and I separated, only my immediate family and one friend knew. Gradually, I told a few other close friends but my wider community didn't hear it from me until five months later, when I shared a positive post on my blog. I wanted to find my way in those early months without feeling I was being watched and I *really* wanted to protect my children and get them used to our new beginning. It remains the best approach I could have taken.

Your situation is personal and *always* your own. So never get drawn into talking about it if you don't wish to. You'll know the people who are sincere, who really care about your wellbeing. They're the ones who drop a lovely, unobtrusive little note through your door, asking if you need anything and just letting you know they're there for you.

Do it your way. Take your time. Find your allies.

They won't necessarily be the people you expected to find standing by your side. But, oh my, they'll be wonderful human beings that will have a place in your heart forever.

Learning 11
I PROTECT MYSELF

'Saying nothing, My Aunt Katie, sometimes says the Most.
There Marauds a sorer Robber, – Silence is his name –
No assault, nor any Menace
Doth betoken him.'

EMILY DICKINSON, IN A LETTER TO HER AUNT

During my silence, a few people speculated about my situation, especially after my eldest had nonchalantly told one of her peers about 'Daddy's flat'.

No one asked me directly, until the occasion when someone confronted me at the school gates – in front of my children – and casually said, 'I'm sorry to hear about your separation,' before clearly wanting to pry further.

The concern wasn't genuine; I knew that instinctively. And, despite usually being very open with people – often sharing too much simply because I didn't know how *not* to share when someone asked me something personal – this time my barriers went up and I shut down the conversation quickly, politely but unapologetically.

I gained a very important learning that day, which was that it is perfectly permissible to protect myself without fear of offending others. I never have to explain my personal circumstances just because someone has asked me to. Until that moment I'm not sure I'd ever actively exercised that entitlement to discretion.

Not once afterwards did I wish I had handled it differently. Not once did I worry what that person must have thought about my reaction. Not once.

Instead I respected that inner voice, which prompted me to stand my ground unequivocally, and I vowed to listen to it more often.

Learning 12

I ALLOW
FOR MORE

Many things worked out as I planned them to, but that
did all not always prove a benefit to me. But almost
everything developed naturally and by destiny.

CARL JUNG, *MEMORIES, DREAMS, REFLECTIONS*

One of the most liberating aspects of my separation for me has been reaffirming the person I always felt I was. Before my marriage challenged the core of my being and changed that perception.

Growing up, I always thought I was destined for certain things. A good job. A big love; the lightning-bolt kind. So it was discouraging when I realized those things had passed me by. Or rather, upon reflection, that *I'd* passed them by. After all, it was my choices that had led me there.

Others were very supportive of my separation. No one believed I should go back; that helped me a lot. People said such nice and encouraging words, which enabled me to access the bravery I needed to find in order to master the adjustment in front of me.

'This isn't the sort of thing parents do when their kids are so young. They usually wait until their children are teenagers and then they split.'

I heard that from some people, and it made me realize that I had begun to see myself as someone who wouldn't accept less than I was worth, because I had sought and enforced change despite the challenges of doing so while having three children under the age of seven. Even if you didn't seek the change, you are allowing for *more* by the very act of accepting and living your new situation, while others look on in awe (I promise you).

When I revisited how I saw myself, and especially when others pointed out my strength, I felt good. I felt strong. *Really* strong. And I began to like the person I saw. More than I had in years.

She was that aspirational girl I remembered growing up with.

And I knew then that it wasn't too late to get the things that *I'd* passed by.

Because I was already allowing for them.

Learning 13

I SEE THAT THERE ARE ALL KINDS OF FAMILIES

'Some families have one mommy, some families have one daddy...and they may not see each other for days, or weeks, months.... But if there's love, dear...those are the ties that bind, and you'll have a family in your heart, forever.'

MRS DOUBTFIRE

When you have children, separation adds another layer of emotions. Because you aren't only dealing with your own, you're also coping with their feelings about what's happened and then your response to those: sadness; guilt; regret.

In the early months, at least, navigating separation with children involved can feel complicated and it can be heartbreaking. During such times it has taken all my resolve to trust that this is the best scenario for us all. But actually, it's the *only* scenario for us all, because it's the one we are living; and resisting it just causes more suffering and conflict.

Until recently I believed that, given the choice, my kids would rather have their parents together than apart. It's how we are conditioned. It's how society tells us a family *should* operate, but the truth is that there are all kinds of families.

And, just as I've grown and moved on during the past four years, so have they, and I'm not sure they *would* choose to go back now. They have reaped huge rewards from our situation.

I also love that my children's beliefs are being challenged through our situation, that they will be freer of damaging stereotypes and social conditioning and instead grow up knowing that *every* way of living as a family unit is 'valid'. Four years on, they no longer say, 'But we want to be a normal family' or 'Why can't you and Daddy live together again?' because they have learned in a very short time that we *are* still a real family, just as we are. This is our new 'normal'.

Of course, there are moments when as a parent I have doubted this, where I have romanticized what had been (see Learning 30) or where I have blamed myself. I am getting better at *not* doing this. Because I know that my only path going forwards is to tune out those thoughts and instead to align myself with what I'm *giving* my children.

> 'You are teaching your kids something I can never. That leaving a man can be the most empowering thing in your life. Never stay with someone because society thinks you should. You're the epitome of a strong woman. And your girls will thank you endlessly one day.'
>
> **A** HAPPILY MARRIED FRIEND

My children will know that anything is possible *because of us* – my ex-husband and me. And even if your separation was not your choice, in the long term you have an opportunity to show your children that human beings can thrive in all kinds of circumstances. Unexpected and otherwise.

For now, we must keep believing in ourselves and in our paths as parents, which have so far led us here.

Learning 14

I DID EVERYTHING TO SAVE MY RELATIONSHIP

'The moment of surrender is not when
life is over. It's when it begins.'
MARIANNE WILLIAMSON, *A RETURN TO LOVE*

At some point in the early days of separation (and occasionally beyond), you may have a moment of doubt, when you question how you ended up in this situation (even if you've done the work to recognize and understand how it all happened).

Maybe you could have tried a little harder. Maybe you could have done things differently. Maybe, maybe, maybe...

This is normal and can happen regardless of how your relationship ended. Even if your partner betrayed you, you may still try to find a way of making yourself accountable, of wondering what you could have done differently.

This type of accountability isn't the empowering kind that we talked about in Learning 2. It's fed by deep regret because, at this very moment, for whatever reason, you don't want to be here. You want to go back. It's also human nature, especially a woman's nature, to feel guilty and to keep playing alternative scenarios over in your mind.

Just stop for a moment and quieten your mind, now.

I do this by telling myself, 'I did everything to save my relationship.' Because I know that I absolutely did. I am guessing you did, too. After all, you're reading this book because you want to learn more about yourself and you want to grow; these are not the actions of someone who does not try or does not love. It just wasn't being mirrored back to you, for whatever reason.

So when we could no longer save our relationships, the only thing left to do was to save ourselves. And we have been doing this, so earnestly, every single day since.

PART 2

MOTIVATION

ENCOURAGING YOURSELF
TO KEEP GOING

Even with the best intentions, there will be days when separation is stifling. When you just don't know how you are going to keep going.

We must never feel ashamed or disappointed when we feel like this. It's normal. It's natural. It's part of the very important grieving process and part of moving on.

What we cannot allow is for such days to disarm us, or make us believe that we've lost everything we've gained so far and we're back to the beginning. We're not. Far from it, in fact. The stumbling blocks we find ourselves facing on the tricky days will, once we've hurdled them, propel us further forwards. And, in the meantime, there are always things we can do to make the challenging moments more bearable.

The next 13 learnings in this second part will show you how I did this.

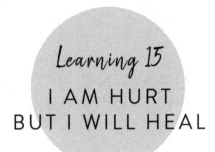

Learning 15
I AM HURT
BUT I WILL HEAL

'What you are developing is a healing attitude.'

DEEPAK CHOPRA, *THE DEEPER WOUND*

Some days hurt. There is no getting away from that. We cannot always put aside our feelings of lack, our perception of failure, or the cruel reality of betrayal.

I knew my marriage was over. I wanted it to be over. I couldn't even think of any reasons to torture myself with 'what if...?' regrets. I didn't want him to fight for me, or for us. Yet every now and then I have still felt sad, hurt and rejected. So if you didn't actually want your relationship to be over, such feelings will only be compounded.

At a psychological level, according to Abraham Maslow's *Hierarchy of Needs*, humans need safety and security, love and belonging, and self-esteem. I have certainly found this to be true in my life, so far.

Separation strikes at the very core of these needs. It takes away the security you thought you knew and the safety of being with someone. There is a void where once there was love and suddenly it isn't clear where you belong. And, especially if the relationship was toxic in some way, your self-esteem might be so low that you feel completely worthless, as I did.

The first thing I remember when I find myself in pain is this: I have every reason to feel hurt and every justification to let myself actually feel it. It is okay.

Then, when I've had time to do this – allowing ourselves periods to do this can be cathartic and illuminating – I notice that the pain feels a little less intense than it did the last time I felt this way.

Every time we go into this place of intense hurt and come out again, I think we learn a little more from our response to that emotion or circumstance and come back brighter, sharper, wiser and more quickly. Every time.

> *'The pent-up energies of anger, fear, and*
> *grief want to find a way out.'*
>
> DEEPAK CHOPRA, *THE DEEPER WOUND*

We see that we are healing, even if the progress is slow. We see that it feels better not to dwell on the hurt. And we see that there has been respite in between these periods and that each time this respite has gradually grown longer. We are developing a new belief system.

Some days may hurt, yes. But they also show us that we will heal.

Because we have already begun.

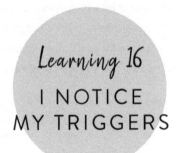

Learning 16
I NOTICE
MY TRIGGERS

Sometimes, when we find ourselves reacting negatively to our separation, the triggers aren't actually coming from within us.

A song on the radio. A smell. A visual representation of what we perceive we no longer have, such as the sight of a smiling couple, lost in each other, walking along hand in hand, or a passing glimpse of a family eating Sunday lunch together in a restaurant. We're suddenly voyeurs where once we were participants.

Our sensory system is finely tuned and, often without even realizing we are doing it, we can find ourselves interpreting and reacting physically to things that are going on around us. Before we know it, something triggers a sinking feeling and sense of loss, possibly spiralling down into a catastrophic (and incorrect) conclusion about our destiny: *I am never going to have that, ever again.*

It's helpful if, in the early months at least, we take note of such triggers as they happen, so we can be aware and work through them. If you know, for example, that a certain situation – such as a social occasion, a place or a date – is going to be painful, you can acknowledge this beforehand and make a conscious choice whether to engage with it or not and prepare yourself, either way.

People talk about facing triggers and working through the pain because avoidance doesn't lead to true healing. However, we *are* allowed to protect ourselves while we are feeling vulnerable, as long as we acknowledge that this is what we're doing and why we're doing it. There is time enough to 'get back out there', in whatever form, as and when you're ready. Alternatively, you could try a different approach and consciously decide to tune out the negative message you're feeding yourself, replace it with one rooted in a healthier emotion (such as gratitude), and go forwards in strength. For example: you don't have to miss out on a party just because 'it will be mostly couples'; go because it's a party and 'there are going to be lovely people there I'd like to catch up with.'

That might take time to achieve but just know that you can do it, any time you choose.

For the time being, remind yourself that you come first and trust your soul to tell you what you need. As we mentioned in Part 1, embracing our own physical space is never to be feared.

On the contrary, it can provide a great source of comfort and offer the greatest clarity.

Learning 17

I DON'T HAVE TO FIRE ON ALL CYLINDERS

'What momentum says is: once you get going in that direction,
it is more likely that you will continue in that direction.'

ABRAHAM HICKS

Going through transitions and new experiences can take its toll on us, mentally and physically.

Often during times of change, when we actually need to look after ourselves the most, we end up depleted. We don't eat well enough, or hydrate regularly. Sleep patterns might be erratic due to intrusive thoughts that just won't leave our minds. Our headspace might feel foggy, as we try to process and make sense of our emotions. We prioritize other people's demands of us over our own needs; it feels imperative that we don't let them down.

Of course, none of these things are conducive to us firing on all cylinders, as we might usually do. And that can make us feel worse – guilty even.

Well, that's okay, because we don't have to fire on all cylinders. Expecting anything of yourself when you're up against it just adds more pressure. Why do this to yourself when what you need now is kindness? From the person who has your back more than anyone else. You.

Now is the time to lean back and trust – in yourself, in the healing ability of time passing, and in the truth you know deep down: that you *will* be okay.

And while you allow that to happen, do things that help your soul start to soar. Notice and appreciate the small things that are actually not small at all, such as the fact you're still breathing, and still have a roof over your head. This will begin to create a momentum of awareness and gratitude.

Then start to build gently upon that momentum, in whatever way feels appealing to you. You might not *really* feel like reading a book, watching a film or going for a walk or run. But what happens when you actually do any of those things? Do you notice a little flutter of hope within? That tingly feeling where you feel just a *little* bit alive again, no matter how little that bit is? It's a small start to building up momentum in the right direction and firing up those cylinders again. The things that seem really, really overwhelming can wait. Apply less force and resistance and more compassion and gentle action. You'll know when you feel more clear-headed and able to tackle the bigger stuff.

And you will. Because what I can promise you now is that some day, not that far away, you are going to relaunch yourself.

Leaving a trail of smoke in your wake.

Learning 18
I WILL PUT ONE FOOT IN FRONT OF THE OTHER

'All I do is keep on running in my own cosy,
homemade void, my own nostalgic silence.
And this is a pretty wonderful thing.'

HARUKI MURAKAMI,
WHAT I TALK ABOUT WHEN I TALK ABOUT RUNNING

Thinking takes up a lot of our energy. Most of us don't even realize how much we overthink and procrastinate in our own lives.

We get so caught up living with an active mind we forget that, with practice, we can start to override our thoughts simply by giving them less airtime. With practice, we can actually just get on with *doing* instead.

Separation while having three children has taught me this. I know that I cannot do everything that needs doing. I simply don't have the woman-power. Ironically, this has made me more proactive, in many ways. An 'all-or-nothing' person from birth, I never did anything in moderation. 'What's the point in doing something, if you can't do it perfectly or completely?' is what I once would have said.

Yet, just as I know I can't do *everything*, I also know that if I do *nothing*, I'll be in exactly the same position as I am right now. So I complete one task, without feeling overwhelmed that I can't do *all* of the to-do list. And afterwards, I don't feel guilty or disappointed that there are still 17 things on the list. I feel quite proud of myself that I managed to achieve *something*, even if it was only putting away the basket of washing that has sat on the kitchen table all week.

Putting one foot in front of the other – without overthinking or challenging ourselves – is really quite liberating. Because we *can* do the thing we want or need to do. The active mind is just telling us otherwise. But if we treat our minds like a computer or iPad and just switch if off, we're left with the ability to function on a very basic task-driven level.

The same goes for navigating our way through our new relationship status. One foot in front of the other. Today doesn't have to be amazing in every way for us to realize when it gradually begins to feel a little better.

We're heading in the direction of our new future.

And, as long as we keep walking (or running, if you're so inclined), that's all that matters.

Learning 19

I WILL FOCUS ON THE NEXT 10 MINUTES

'Life is always in motion so you cannot be stuck.'

ESTHER HICKS

S ome days, no matter how good the day before was or how much progress we feel we made, we wake up feeling stuck.

This can set us back, if we let it. It can take us to that catastrophic place where we feel like this is *never* going to get easier. How can it? It was okay yesterday. Surely today should be even better? That's how progress works, isn't it?

And yet, we *know* it doesn't work like that.

As I mentioned, for a whole year after my separation, I flew. The good stuff just kept coming and I felt amazing. Pretty much all of the time.

After I crashed – actually it was more of a sudden collision between my ideal world and my reality – I have *never* been as consistently high as in that first year. Sometimes I feel really stuck. The more it happens, the more I'm understanding its purpose and what it's teaching me, and the more I'm allowing it to just happen rather than desperately trying to fix it so I can get on with feeling amazing again. I also know that tomorrow will very likely *not* be a day of feeling stuck. Remember what we said in Learning 9, about how ultimately it gets easier to trust in the feeling of being okay.

'Focus on raising your mood in the next 10 minutes,' a friend said to me once, when I was struggling. 'Do something nice or even something mundane to distract yourself.'

So I did. And what happened? I didn't suddenly soar above the clouds. But I did feel better. Because I reclaimed *my* power to change my current vibration. It reminded me that I *always* have the power to do this. Me. Not anyone else. Me.

Focusing on the next 10 minutes remains one of the most effective techniques I employ, whenever I just can't move forwards or the bigger picture is out of focus. What works for me, lifts my mood, and always gets me moving forwards is focusing on something mundane that I've been putting off – mopping the floor, putting away that washing (yes, truly) – anything that halts my thoughts for a moment and moves me into a different energy field. Running, followed by a well-earned coffee or treat, has a similar effect. It's about figuring out what works for you and doing it, without protest. That's the key.

Because the next 10 minutes is all any of us can *really* influence.

And when we only think about those 10 minutes, it dissipates all the pressure and anxiety associated with an uncertain and daunting future and makes us feel like we can do anything. Which, of course, we *can*.

Learning 20

I WILL BELIEVE WHAT OTHERS SEE IN ME

'Sometimes you can't see yourself clearly until you see yourself through the eyes of others.'

ELLEN DEGENERES

If you've ever had someone in your corner, who truly and consistently believes in you, you'll know what a powerful incentive this is to keep going, with pride.

It is not always easy to see the good in ourselves. We aren't practiced at doing so. When it comes to a situation like separation, in which we may have been rejected at the hands of someone else, it can be nigh on impossible. *There* must *be something wrong with me*, you might find yourself thinking. We can even find ourselves believing this if the separation was our choice, particularly if our partner moves on quickly and finds someone else with whom they appear to be much happier. *Why didn't they want me?*

Once we get into this mindset – and it is very normal – it can be hard to extract ourselves. The negative self-talk perpetuates more, and before we know it we have created an entirely new persona that isn't us, at all.

While we must ultimately learn to nurture our own self-esteem (we'll look at this in Part 5), in the early days it really helps to have cheerleaders who believe in us and can give us a boost and a word of encouragement when we need it. Ask those close to you for support; don't be embarrassed. They'll be so honoured you did.

And, although you may not recognize yourself in this person they speak of so encouragingly, whom they hold so dear, right now you don't have to. Just trust that they *know* you. They love you. They see you better than you can see yourself right now.

Believe what they see in you. You'll be back really soon, to see for yourself.

Learning 21
I WILL BE KIND TO MYSELF

'If I cannot live with myself there must be two of me: the "I" and the "self" that "I" cannot live with. "Maybe," I thought, "only one of them is real."'

ECKHART TOLLE, *THE POWER OF NOW*

It's a buzz phrase, these days: 'Be kind to yourself.' But what does it really mean?

On a physical level, it might mean looking after ourselves: self-care (another buzz phrase). Eating better. Exercising. Having a bath. All things that any of us can, and deserve to, do.

Yet showing kindness to ourselves has to run deeper than this. And it is often much harder to do than simply running a bath. This is because our egos get in the way – that ego being any image we have of ourselves that gives us an inaccurate sense of identity, usually derived from the things we tell ourselves and the things other people say about us that we've decided to accept as truth.

Our egos aren't *real* but are a creation of too many thoughts, influences and goals. Ego acts mostly from fear, irritation, anger, impatience and sadness. It tries to get us to act, criticize and separate ourselves from those around us. It likes us to be 'better' than others and it will do anything to achieve this end. So when it comes to being kind to ourselves, ego is a huge obstacle: because it behaves like an overbearing parent judging and berating us; because we haven't done as well as we should have done. It prevents us from connecting with our inner child – that child who has been there since our birth and still needs looking after, just as we would hopefully look after any *actual* child.

How crazy is this? That we listen so intently and rely so much on something that isn't even real. We trust it.

So, for me, being kind to myself is reaching beyond my ego, way beyond what I am or did or didn't do, and loving myself no matter what (more about this in Learning 76). I have started to visualize putting my ego away in a box or having my soul flying above me, watching and guiding me when my ego is stubborn and wants to take hold. Because sometimes it helps to have a tangible image, and my soul is always a more reliable guide than my ego.

Learning to love ourselves is what each of us deserves. This is especially important during separation, when your ego might perceive the end of your relationship as a failure or some sort of inadequacy on your part.

So don't ever listen to any inner voice that attacks you. That's not coming from your soul. From *you*.

Instead, reach deep, choose kind words, observe how you speak to yourself and nurture your inner child.

Souls don't create anger or hate. Egos do.

Learning 22
I WILL
ASK FOR HELP

*'Nothing alleviates suffering like reaching out
to another person who is suffering.'*
DEEPAK CHOPRA, *THE DEEPER WOUND*

In the early months of my separation, I was shown just how many others surrounded me as a force field of friendship.

They weren't necessarily the people I expected to see standing by my side. But they were people who positioned themselves in such a way that I knew they were there.

This was *really* important while I was finding my feet. It meant I knew there were others I could ask for help if I needed it or if I was having a tricky day. And I did ask occasionally.

Asking, I've found, is not the same as putting your hand up and saying, 'I can't cope'. I *can* cope. So can you. It's just that, today, we're going to do it with a little company. There's nothing wrong with that.

Also, when we give others an opportunity to help us, it doesn't just help us; it also helps *them*. Because it connects us with a transmission of lovely, compassionate energy that lifts receiver *and* giver.

These connections have been the greatest pleasure of my separation. Now, I seek them everywhere and with everyone. Not just when I'm with close friends. But at the school gates. At the checkout. With a passing stranger. Because I see that how we behave and how we are with each other *matters*: the words we employ, the gestures we make. I have been lifted by the kindness or warmth of a stranger. It changes *everything*. And it might be a stranger's turn to deserve that.

When we connect from a place of love, we raise one another's vibrational energy. And that is contagious. It attracts more of the same. And it has a domino effect way beyond your personal interaction.

That has the power to change everything.

Amidst the busy lives we all lead, it's possible to think we aren't in tune with one another any more. But that doesn't mean that no one is listening. Someone always is.

And it doesn't take much to ignite. So, if you're struggling, tell someone. Anyone. Pick up the phone. Meet a friend for a coffee. Confide in the cashier. Break down if you need to. You'll feel so much better for talking things through. Pay it back and be the person who spares the time to really listen, who gives *someone else* an opportunity to talk things through, without trying to fix them.

We all desire this human connection and whomever you talk to will be as grateful as you are for the opportunity to share and be comforted.

We care when you're having a tricky time. And when we're aware, we'll do whatever we can to help.

You only have to ask.

(Please make sure you do.)

Learning 23

I DRAW STRENGTH FROM OTHERS WHO UNDERSTAND

'It helps when one recognizes our shared humanity.'

DOUGLAS ABRAMS, FROM *THE BOOK OF JOY*

Sharing a word with someone in a similar situation to us can be a source of incredible strength.

As a separated parent, I have found that no one else *really* gets my circumstances like another separated parent. How could they? Why should they?

I remember a conversation I had with the receptionist at the swimming pool, as I rang off from speaking curtly to my ex-husband. 'I recognize that conversation,' she said with an empathetic smile.

She didn't have to say anything more. Those four words spoke volumes. 'I understand and I *know*.' They made me remember, in that moment that I needed to be reminded, that I'm not alone in the challenges I face as a solo parent.

Empathy – receiving *and* giving – is empowering. It strengthens us. It's the power of that human connection again. It's one of the better reasons we share our lives on social media.

We all seek to be understood. To belong. Somewhere.

Our ultimate goal is to be able to soar without these validations from others; *this* I know. But I also recognize that there are times when a little empathy and encouragement give us that extra boost to allow us to take off.

So we can return to flying.

Learning 24
I AM
NEVER ALONE

'Awareness is learning to keep yourself company'
GENEEN ROTH, *BREAKING FREE FROM EMOTIONAL EATING*

Separation can feel lonely, until we understand that it is only our perception that makes it so.

If we source ultimate meaning in being half of someone else, we have forgotten that we were already whole to begin with.

When my ex-husband moved out, I was fortunate enough to still live with my three children. I was literally *never* alone, and yet there were times where I felt desperately lonely – mainly when I tortured myself with thoughts of other couples and families, living happily around me, if only in my imagination.

The physical longing for another human being was palpable. To be held. To be understood. To have the loving touch of another (who wasn't two years old and slightly sticky).

As I began to put myself back together and become *whole* once more, this longing decreased. I still really wanted some strong arms around me but that was something I desired, rather than a factor I couldn't live without.

As long as I was aligned, I didn't feel the intensity of loneliness. I became accustomed to – and even enjoyed – my own company in the evenings and when the children went to stay with their dad (see Learning 70). I stopped associating *being alone* with being lonely. One did not have to equal the other.

I am not a loner because I am alone.

Those were never my words, anyway. They were society's, the media's, the people around me who couldn't imagine being single, alone or without their other half.

When we start to view ourselves as a whole, now and always, as someone who doesn't *need* another (and the rest of this book will look at *how* we might do this), we are choosing never to be alone in the 'lonely' sense.

There is no greater state than separation, in my opinion, to show us this truth.

When you are everything to you, you are in perfect alignment with yourself holding your vibration, regardless of what happens around you.

Then, everything and everyone else becomes icing and sprinkles on the amazing cake you already are.

Learning 25
I WILL
SUPPORT OTHERS

*'No one is useless in this world who lightens
the burden of it for any one else.'*
CHARLES DICKENS, *OUR MUTUAL FRIEND*

When my friend found herself separated with two small children and a baby on the way, I was able to support her because of what I had been through with my own separation, even though our circumstances were vastly different.

I could see right then, even though she couldn't, that she was going to be just fine, without any help from me or others. Despite the heartbreak, I could see the strength she possessed inside. She continues to amaze me.

One year on, she was soaring. She still is. She says she couldn't have got through it without her friends, 'You gave me hope.'

She did, of course, do it all by herself. But I know the sense of gratitude she feels. I have it too for all the people who took – and still take – the time to have my back. I always will.

And it is worth noting that what you are navigating now is, one day, going to support someone else. Your pain is going to help heal another's. It might seem unfathomable at this very moment, but it's true. *You* are going to make a difference. Isn't that incredible?

There are amazing people on this planet who have the gift of empathy or learned skills in listening without having to experience every single one of life's scenarios.

And then there is *you*. Who is going to make someone else feel better.

Just by *being* you.

Learning 26
I WILL
LOOK FOR PEACE

'The ego says, "Once everything falls into place, I'll feel peace."
The spirit says, "Find your peace, and then
everything will fall into place."'

MARIANNE WILLIAMSON

In the First Noble Truth, Buddha introduces us to the idea that pain is certain but suffering (*dhukka*) is optional. It's true that, sometimes at least, we can simply (or not so simply – it does take practice) opt *not* to suffer, by choosing not to engage with our pain and taking our focus elsewhere to attract a different vibration.

The vibration of peace.

Where does peace exist for you? Have you ever even thought about that? When was the last time you *actually* felt it?

For me, the combination of nature and exercise has always provided my purest moments of joy and peace. Lying under a big open sky.

Running in my favourite park. Noticing the trees and feeling the ground beneath my feet. Watching the sea crest and trough. Being in the presence of historical, natural beauty that has survived a million more catastrophes than I ever will.

Reminding myself that I am just one minuscule living organism in a huge, majestic universe always makes me feel more peaceful and gracious. It diminishes my problems. It quietens my mind. It takes me *out* of my head, where I sometimes spend so much time living.

Your peace will be different but it's worth giving it some consideration and actively seeking it out, just as we do so easily and naturally with suffering. Learn to just *be*.

Since my separation, I am much more comfortable just *being*. I am less concerned with analysing and fixing, and happier accepting what *is*. There are some things that just don't need an explanation or answer *right now*, or possibly ever.

And therein lies peace, if only for a moment.

Learning 27

I WILL NOTICE LOVE IN ALL ITS MANY FORMS

'Love is insid you. Love is evree wer.'

Ivy Ransom (aged six)

Love. A word that for many of us probably conjures up an image of a romantic love that is meant to complete us.

And yet, if we don't find romantic love, or we 'settle' and live with a compromised version of love, or we lose it altogether – what does this mean? That we are never to be happy (again)? That we are never to *know* love (again)?

When my then six-year-old drew me a picture of a heart with the words, 'Love is insid you. Love is evree wer,' I saw that she had already grasped something that I, and so many others, have long forgotten.

Firstly, 'Love is inside you.' Self-love. The ability to dig deep and love ourselves, from within and without question. This isn't narcissism, because you don't seek to share your view of yourself with the world in order for it to exist. It is the ultimate unconditional love and the one that will serve us forever, because it only depends upon us to thrive. We will look at this much more in Part 5.

Secondly, 'Love is everywhere.' The vibrational energy we can all share, if we allow it to flow freely. The more love you radiate, the more love comes back to you. It's in our family and friends, of course. Our children, if we have them. But I have also noticed myself feeling it with complete strangers because their words or actions came from a place of love.

Love. We need to redefine its meaning and its source.

Because love *is* inside you and it *is* everywhere.

PART 3

INSIGHT

UNDERSTANDING YOURSELF
THROUGH SEPARATION

From an early age, we are told that life is about hitting desirable and socially acceptable milestones. First steps. Starting school. Graduation. The first job. First home. Finding love. Perhaps marriage and children. Promotion. A bigger home. A better job.

The striving never ends.

Nowhere in that list do we find separation or divorce. And yet, for me and countless others, separation has been one of the most important and liberating milestones of all.

It has shown me far more about myself than anything before, with the exception, perhaps, of motherhood.

And it has been such an unexpected gift to have had an opportunity to get to know myself and look deeper at myself, in particular the areas in which I wish to grow.

Separation has given me another chance at me. And these next 11 learnings will show how.

Learning 28
I CAN MAKE UP STORIES IN MY HEAD

*'If you don't know, ask. You will be a fool for the
moment, but a wise man for the rest of your life.'*

SENECA THE YOUNGER

Some time ago, I was listening to a podcast with Brené Brown, author of *Daring Greatly*. She was talking about disagreements with her husband and how, because she often interprets them only from her perspective, she interprets them inaccurately. 'I'm making up the story in my head right now,' she tells him, which gives her husband the opportunity to put the other side of that story, correct her interpretation, and immediately resolve the argument or lack of communication before it escalates.

That phrase really struck a chord with me: 'I'm making up the story in my head right now.' Because I used to do this *all the time*, especially in my marriage. I still do it *some* of the time, but I am now aware when I do.

In the past I've thought I knew what someone else was thinking or what their motivation was, and this would then shape my response. But my reaction wouldn't be accurate, of course, because I'd interpreted only from my perspective; I'd made the whole thing up.

We all have the ability to do this and, if you've ever analysed a conversation after you've had it, you'll know how inaccurate the replay can be and how much energy you can expend misinterpreting it.

We can never know how someone else is feeling unless *they* tell us. Everything else we *think* we know are stories our egos tell us, either to make ourselves feel better or to try and force a solution.

Knowing you might do this is extremely helpful in the throes of separation, especially if you're still in communication with your ex-partner. That awareness can stop you spiralling, mentally, because it can help you avoid winding yourself up with a chain of antagonistic thoughts as you attempt to analyse and understand your ex-partner's behaviour.

If the thought originates in your mind, it's *your* thought. Don't be fooled and assume it's true simply because you thought it. It may just be trying to trick you, as thoughts do.

When we find ourselves in the midst of conflict, we have the opportunity to tell ourselves a different story. One that begins with, 'I don't know why they said or did that but if I *can't* ask, then I owe it to myself, and to them, not to torment myself with works of fiction.'

Remember, it's *your* thought, not theirs.

Learning 29

I AM RESPONSIBLE FOR ALL MY DECISIONS

*'Owning our story and loving ourselves through that
process is the bravest thing that we will ever do.'*

BRENÉ BROWN

The one recurring learning that separation keeps showing me is that I am the only one accountable for every decision I make, or don't make.

There is never anyone else to blame when something doesn't work out because, somewhere along the line, I made a choice or a series of choices that led me here. Every decision, no matter how small, has a consequence. There is a cause and there is an effect.

In Part 1, I talked about the healing power of understanding your role in your separation. Taking responsibility for yourself and your decisions, and realizing that it is *only* you who is sending out your current vibration into the universe, is the ultimate self-admission. Even when that admission feels hard.

And, once you've addressed this, you'll find that it spills out into *every* other area of your life. You don't like the job you have? *You* can do something about that. You want to live in a different way? *You* can put that into place, but only by sending out an alternative vibration and intention.

It is both an empowering and a daunting realization. 'Owning it' always is, and we have all been guilty of creating habits that mean sometimes it feels much better if we can put responsibility onto someone else rather than ourselves. There is less pressure on ourselves to move forwards if we can put a whole host of external obstacles in the way: 'I would do that if...'

Often the thought of making a decision is so daunting that we simply put it off. I used to think this was a negative tactic – procrastination on my part. Now, because I am mostly actively accountable for my life, I realize it's just because I don't know the answer yet. And that's okay. It's worse to force a decision and make one you're not instinctive about because that one decision, made in haste, has the power to create a ripple effect – the consequences of which you could potentially be living with for years to come.

There are of course those times when it's just procrastination, and then I just have to *do something* by putting one foot in front of the other.

But when my path ahead is masked by fog, I do nothing and trust that it will become clear. It always does.

At other times, in contrast, I make a decision instinctively and confidently because I just *know* it's the one to make in that moment.

Either way, the decision is *mine*.

Own *yours*.

Learning 30

I CAN ROMANTICIZE
MY FORMER RELATIONSHIP

*'When I find myself putting that "old" life on a pedestal
and thinking that it was perfect, I try to remember
that this is a romanticized view of the past that serves
only to make me feel bad about the present.'*
TONI BERNHARD, PSYCHOLOGY TODAY BLOG

Mostly, there have been very few occasions on which I have
wondered whether I should try to resurrect my relationship
with my ex-husband.

A couple of these occasions have coincided with nearing the closing
stages of divorce, because I was feeling a sense of finality, tinged with
a little sadness. Although, of course, with three children between us
there will never *really* be finality, at least until they are adults (and
probably not even then).

The other occasions have been purely down to my tendency to romanticize and forget what life together was *really* like, for the sake of sharing our family together, rather than for each other.

That's never a good enough reason.

The mind, I have found, is excellent at creating thoughts based on what it desires in that very moment. So, if it's a Sunday and I am in the park running and passing families scooting and playing happily, or seemingly so, before I know it my mind has wandered away with itself. Suddenly I am seeing my own family's faces on those scooters, wondering when it all fell apart and whether it was *really* that intolerable.

We were like them once, weren't we?

And, of course, we were. Because every relationship has happy and loving times and it is mostly impossible to pinpoint the moment one or both of you just gave up or moved on. It was a series of moments, stretched over time, the conclusion of which you could never have seen coming, until it came.

Then my ex-husband drops the kids back and we find ourselves in each other's company again – he hands me a bag of washing, he utters a couple of monosyllables, and he is gone.

The rose petals that are my imagination fall away, one by one.

And my thoughts return to what I know to be true.

We're not like them, now. And that's okay.

Learning 31

I DO NOT NEED TO COMPARE MY LIFE TO OTHERS

'Being famous on Instagram is like being rich in Monopoly.'

UNKNOWN

Comparison is today's measure of success and it is an unfortunate and destructive barometer. It isn't enough to be doing well on our own terms. We need to know how we stand against others. Quite often, we need to be *better*. Richer. Happier. Fitter.

The world of social media has aggravated the tendency to compare and given us an almost insatiable appetite for it. Other people's success stories. Other people's happy milestones. Other people, full stop.

We obsess about other people's careers, relationships, wardrobes, houses and popularity. We place so much importance in these things that we don't even see how artificial they are. That they are only better, richer, happier or fitter because we perceive them to be so. It isn't *real*.

Comparison relies on our own perception to even exist; if we don't see it and we don't feed it, it can't breathe.

Separation challenges the very practice of comparison because it immediately makes us stand apart from so many of our peers, who are 'more successful' in love than us. This isn't debatable to us; they are still with their partner while we are not. Suddenly, we don't have to compete; we have nothing with which to barter.

It takes time to see what a great blessing this will come to be.

Because we won't have to view someone else's glossy togetherness from a place of uneasiness, knowing our relationship is far from this. And we will learn that comparison is never about wanting someone else's life; it is always about *us* and where we want life to be. It just gets muddled up amidst the plights of others.

And this realization will gradually spill over into every area of our lives, as we learn to channel our energy and intentions in *our* direction, without validating ourselves for the purpose of others (validating *yourself* is a different matter, which we'll look at in Learning 51).

There is never any need to compare, to impress, to compete.

I know that when that noise is quiet, I am happy *as I am* and *with what I have*. I know that my path is *mine* and not anyone else's.

I don't need any more context than that. And neither do you.

Learning 32

I FORGIVE MYSELF

*'Forgiveness is the only way to heal ourselves
and to be free from the past.'*
ARCHBISHOP DESMOND TUTU, FROM *THE BOOK OF JOY*

This is a principle I apply to myself in everyday life – especially when I find myself experiencing inner conflict. I simply choose to forgive myself.

Whatever the circumstances. Whatever my actions. Whatever my words.

I talked about being kind to ourselves in Learning 21, and about how the ego stops us from connecting with and protecting our inner child. The one who needs understanding and forgiveness, always.

If anyone has ever said to you – as they have to me – 'You're so hard on yourself,' this is something for you to work on. It's not easy if for years you've always 'told yourself off'. But it can be done. And it is worth the effort.

Because, in many ways, self-forgiveness is actually the ultimate state of being from which all good will stem: the effect of all the learnings and practices in this book. It's the state in which we never judge or berate ourselves. It's the state in which we can choose to live, in complete alignment.

Forgiveness is showing yourself love. Unconditional love. The type of love we rarely shine inwards. It's looking for the good in *you* and finding it (write a list if it helps to focus you). It's a process which, in turn, nurtures a forgiving acceptance of others.

Whatever the circumstances. Whatever their actions. Whatever their words.

Because we all deserve forgiveness and it begins with us.

I MAKE PROGRESS,
NEVER MISTAKES

*'The only real mistake is the one
from which we learn nothing.'*

HENRY FORD

Failure. Mistakes. Let's just strike those words from our vocabulary now, shall we?

Because, if we really want to change the way we think about separation (and life, come to that), we can simply choose to look at things in a more positive, forgiving way. Forgiving of ourselves, that is.

I could berate myself for marrying someone I probably shouldn't have married. A pretty gigantic 'mistake'. I could interpret everything that followed as further errors, weakening an already feeble infrastructure. I could see the decision to have a third baby as a pretty diabolical gamble. A bet I well and truly lost.

More to the point, so could others.

And yet, sitting here today, nothing feels like a mistake. Least of all my beautiful boy. Every decision I have made and continue to make feels like a stepping stone on a path that is appearing in front of me, as I walk it.

There is so much we can take from every experience – joyful or painful – and the more we allow ourselves to engage fully with these experiences, the more we open ourselves up to our souls, which really believe we can do anything and always encourage us to try.

Our souls, which know we are always making progress, never mistakes.

Learning 34
I DO THIS FOR MY CHILDREN

*'I am prouder of my years as a single mother
than of any other part of my life.'*

J.K. ROWLING

I decided early on that I was going to move forwards positively in my separation. I did this primarily for my children, but ultimately it has benefitted me enormously too. If I was going to inflict this change on them, I simply had to show them that it was going to make their lives better. And it has. It really has.

There are huge benefits to our situation; the amount of time I spend with them, for one. But also the autonomy they've gained, very naturally, because I am often stretched, physically and mentally. We have to do things differently as a one-parent family and I have to afford them more independence because I am only one person and I can only do so much. But, as a result of this, I am seeing them thrive.

They are self-aware and take pride in being part of the special tribe we have created; something I have always encouraged. We talk often about being a team, and I feel closer to my children and more in tune with them than ever before.

They are compassionate beyond their years and, in the absence of my partner, they've taken on the role of caring for me if I've been unwell, exhausted or low. I've heard other parents say they feel guilty when their child has had to do this or has seen them upset or vulnerable. But I believe our children are being given an amazing opportunity to realize that we are vulnerable and it's okay to feel, not resist, this. It's even more enabling for them when they see us come back quickly (see Learning 52).

And then, when I'm wondering if I'm making a mess of it all – because we all have doubtful days – someone comments on the kindness of one of my children. A teacher calls one of them 'captivating' or remarks upon another's smile and positive approach to life.

And I know that we're all doing just fine.

So much better than fine.

(If you have children, be proud. Keep doing this for them.)

Learning 35
I ENJOY
TIME WITHOUT CONFLICT

*'We don't realize that somewhere within us all, there
does exist a supreme self who is eternally at peace.'*
ELIZABETH GILBERT, *EAT, PRAY, LOVE*

For a long time, I was wound up like a tightly sprung coil. I didn't even realize it until the day after my ex-husband moved out, when suddenly my default state of mind was calm.

There was nothing. No tormenting thoughts. No anxiety bubbling away because I was constantly anticipating the inevitable conflict or confusion between us and the fact that there just seemed no way of communicating with one another.

There was just me.

On a practical level, there was no frustration at the fact he wouldn't have done stuff like put the bins out. If you've participated in it, you'll know that the Bin Battle is a very real thing in relationships.

In our house, we used to take turns to see who could fit in just one more grapefruit peel, teabag or nappy (if you won, you passed GO, collected £200 and didn't have to take out the bin). I have friends who are still married and say it often feels so much harder when their partner is there and who envy my autonomy; co-parenting is a skill that certainly takes time to master.

There is a lot to be said for living your life without conflict. You can use your energy on so much more. And, as you do, you bring more and more calm into your life.

You discover that actually you're a peacemaker at heart. You, who was once so fiery.

And going forwards, you opt *not* to embroil yourself in other people's gripes or arguments because you have had enough conflict of your own. You choose gentler words and you avoid engaging in the politics that bubble away under the surface of many groups and communities.

You've seen that there is a different, more preferable way to live.

A peaceful way.

And you start living it.

Learning 36
I AM
ALWAYS LEARNING

'And always, there was the magic of learning things'
BETTY SMITH, *A TREE GROWS IN BROOKLYN*

When we reach adulthood, we expect to know all of the answers to life. Milestones may have been reached. We're getting on with the business of living. Which is possibly the whole concept behind the 'mid-life crisis'.

'Is *this* it?'

Separation stops us in our tracks. Because it forces us to re-evaluate *this*. To change and adapt. We realize we aren't where we thought we'd be. And we don't know as much as we thought. It's the greatest gift we'll ever unwrap, even if we can't immediately get through the reams of tape.

Any major life event has the same effect.

I know this is why separation has injected so much vigour into my life. Had my ex-husband and I stayed together, I simply would not have had all the opportunities to learn that the past four years have given me. And it's a privilege to be starting again but with so many riches that I've gathered along the way. To realize that this *isn't* it.

It's a rebirth.

And it further invigorates me when I hear people in their latter years talk of experiencing and learning, still. Because if we're open and listening, we'll be learning and growing, as we're meant to.

Until the day we die.

(And beyond.)

Learning 37

I DON'T NEED TO KNOW EVERYTHING

'Any fool can know. The point is to understand.'

<small>ALBERT EINSTEIN</small>

In the age of knowing *everything*, being able to have information in a millisecond, and living on social media, it takes some reconditioning to remind ourselves that actually we don't need to know *everything*.

Especially when it comes to someone with whom we were once intimate.

If you've ever whipped yourself up into a frenzy stalking your ex on social media, you'll know where I'm going with this. It never made you feel *better*, did it?

I have learned, through separation, that some things are better left unsaid and unasked. I don't need to know *anything* about my ex-husband's whereabouts now, aside from the agreed times when he is to collect our kids. So I ask nothing and share little about my life, too.

It is not my business any more. And mine is not his.

Because even if, like me, your split was mutual and remains mostly amicable, you are still a human being with feelings. And, some days, you will feel hurt or rejected by your ex. It's natural. You were building a life together. You shared a lot together. You may have been raising children together.

You don't need to aggravate your feelings by digging deeper into their new social life, partner or flamboyant holidays. Stick to looking at random pictures of your friend's grandma's cat at 11:30 p.m. instead.

It's far safer.

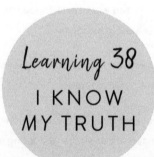

Learning 38
I KNOW MY TRUTH

'The truth is rarely pure and never simple.'
OSCAR WILDE, *THE IMPORTANCE OF BEING EARNEST*

One of the things I have struggled with in the past, and which has raised its head again in separation, is being misunderstood and misinterpreted by others.

As a person who tries to live honestly and truthfully, being misinterpreted has always felt like one of the biggest crimes that could be committed against me.

How did that person not understand my intentions?

If our greatest desire is belonging and not being intrinsically flawed, then being misinterpreted is our greatest fear and obstacle to this.

Separation can be a place of opposing sides: Team You and Team Them. There is much room for speculation and opinion. You want your ex to understand *your* point of view. You want others to know *your* side of the story. You want them to see you as *you* see yourself. You want them to see the good in you.

In time, you discover that this need is impossible to fulfil. And it's unnecessary. You only have to find *your* truth and live it, with devotion.

So, if you're fearful that your ex-mother-in-law has misinterpreted you as The Devil Incarnate or you're wondering why your ex-partner understands you *less* in separation than in partnership, ask yourself if there is any leverage in your perception. Maybe there is, in which case you have a chance to change that truth, for yourself. Or perhaps, you've made up the story in your head again (see Learning 28). Or perhaps, *it just doesn't matter.*

Because is there ever any point in trying to make someone else think another way? *Your* way. That would be a full-time job in itself, leaving you little time to get on with the *real* job in hand.

Knowing *your* truth.

And living it.

PART 4

SELF-EXPRESSION

SHOWING YOURSELF
WHO YOU ARE

Expressing ourselves is something that many of us aren't accomplished at doing.

In a world in which, increasingly, we measure ourselves against others or we worry about what others may think of us, we have simply forgotten that we are able to express ourselves authentically. And we must, if we are to align fully with ourselves.

Separation provides an incredible opportunity in which to do this. It prompts us to ask the questions: 'What do I want?'; 'How do I feel about this?'; 'Why am I doing it this way?'

It challenges our belief system that others matter more than us. It puts us back into the centre of our own lives.

These next 15 learnings are the primary ways in which I began to align *myself* with *me*.

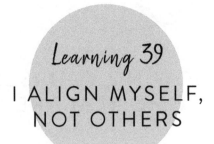

Learning 39
I ALIGN MYSELF, NOT OTHERS

'Your relationship with your inner being is what matters most.'

ABRAHAM HICKS

Many of us who concern ourselves with the lives or wellbeing of others do so without realizing that it is not our responsibility to secure anyone's good fortune but our own. We are doing both ourselves *and* others a disservice whenever we try to do this.

We can be kind and look out for others, but it is not up to *us* to make them happy, secure or whatever it is they seek. Likewise, it is not up to *them* to make us happy, secure or whatever it is that we seek.

And it is actually impossible.

My marriage demonstrated this, as I looked for my ex-husband to fulfil my 'happiness' and tried to align (read: 'change') him in the process. My separation, in all its illuminating glory, revealed the impossibility of achieving this, at which point I realized that I can only align myself.

My three children continue to remind me of this on a daily basis. In my experience there is nothing like motherhood, when you are so often at the 'mercy' of others, to challenge your ability to hold your vibration (by which I mean: to keep your energy and intentions stable and in alignment with you). The author Eckhart Tolle says that being a parent provides a greater opportunity than meditation for reaching consciousness.

Because remaining in alignment with myself, rather than with them and their rapidly changing moods and experiences, takes continual awareness and practice on my part. This is especially true in the mornings, for example, when I am trying not to become frustrated at the disarray that is still often present in the school-run routine – despite the fact that we have been doing it for years – and I can react against my intentions by micro-managing it. On some days, I can lean back and I see how far I've come in ten years as a mother; I see that I am conscious, aware and in alignment. But on other days, when I have temporarily let that awareness slip, my children remind me that I still have far to go in aligning myself, not them. I am grateful to them for their guidance.

I align myself, not others.

On another level, they unwittingly teach me why it is *never* my role to make someone else's world 'right'. They look to me to resolve the issues in their lives – sibling squabbles, fulfilling their desires, alleviating their dissatisfaction or boredom – but these are impossible tasks to resolve for them and to try does little to nurture our children. It teaches them to rely on others, not themselves, the only one they ever truly need. It's the same with the adults in our lives.

We try to swing the rapidly oscillating pendulum of our child's mood from anger or disappointment towards joy and elation because it makes us – the parent – feel uncomfortable to do nothing. But any parent who's been at a checkout unable to resist their child's urgent demands – 'I have to have this toy/sweets *now!*' – only to be confronted by yet another equally urgent but completely different demand moments later, knows there is no real salvation in this approach. If we just let it happen, with awareness, we can create an opportunity for our children to learn to align themselves.

'*You* can make yourself happy,' I tell my children. '*You* can figure this out.' And usually they do, and they can. Children instinctively align themselves, not others. It is us parents and adults who take this away from them, over time, as we insist that they 'do' rather than 'be'. Or we simply do it for them.

We don't all have children, but we do all have catalysts. An ex-partner, certainly. Friends. Family. Colleagues.

If you're a people-pleaser or preoccupied with what others think of you, it can be challenging not to try and align others; so much of your self-actualization is reliant on them liking you or on their perception of you.

But once you see that aligning others is an impossible proposition and one that only limits *you*, you can start to live more freely and focus on the process that will ultimately bring you everything you desire.

Aligning *you*.

Learning 40
I MAKE
MY OWN RULES

*'I'm not going to limit myself just because people won't
accept the fact that I can do something else.'*

DOLLY PARTON

grew up with order. Structure. Boundaries. I see now that I have
relied upon these all my life, to make *sense* of my life.

If I didn't do things in the 'right' way, I felt sure I wouldn't 'succeed'.
The opposite turned out to be true (more about this myth in
Learning 42).

The truth is, I have come to learn that having too many rules and plans
results in me living my life *out* of alignment. They make me unhappy
and, conversely, more chaotic because I feel the pressure of fulfilling
them. They tease me to try and be that consistent being I simply
cannot be (and don't need to be). They make me want to rebel. Being
consistent isn't necessary, for any of us, and is where our suffering so
often comes from.

I'm also not sure *who* I've been obeying the rules *for*.

Separation liberated me, immediately, because it struck at the very core of the order and relationship model I'd known: my parents are still married, after 50 years.

It showed me that I could be okay, making my own new rules for me and my family. Making your own rules is invigorating.

I don't deny that we need some structure and order to stop civilization descending into chaos. Children certainly respond to boundaries. But I'm also sure we can achieve the same outcomes if we root our efforts in instinct and love rather than in rigid rules that we've ceased to understand or that no longer work for our present circumstances.

I still have a level of order in my life, of course. We all need to eat, sleep and exercise. But it is flexible. I don't impose or obey rules for the sake of them. In fact, in our house there's just one: 'Be a team.'

(Oh, and: '*Please* pick your pants up off the floor.')

Learning 41

I AM THE CREATOR OF MY SELF-ESTEEM

'Self-esteem comes from being able to define the world in your own terms and refusing to abide by the judgement of others.'

OPRAH WINFREY

Separation shatters self-esteem, but then it rebuilds it taller and stronger than it has ever stood before.

For separation teaches us that never again will our definition of 'self' rely upon anything or anyone but *ourselves*.

Our self-esteem is present in everything that we say and do. The vocabulary we use, our tone, our body language and our actions. It is not easy, or natural, for everyone to believe in themselves, and Part 5 will look at how we do this.

It is even harder to have self-belief if you've been in a relationship in which you were being criticized, especially if you didn't even realize it was happening. This is where real damage can be done, because the messaging is so subliminal it simply starts to become a part of you: *who you are now*. You didn't open the door and invite it in, you didn't see it cross over the threshold and you didn't realize it was redefining you in the process.

By the end of my marriage, I had come to believe that I was unattractive and not very capable. My light had gone out and my self-esteem had been remoulded by how my ex-husband appeared to see me.

I had *allowed* this, because I was seeing myself *only* through his eyes.

It took separation to open mine and show me that I *was* capable. I *am* capable.

I *am*.

Your inner voice is quietly greater than anyone else's; anyone who *tries* to shout louder, who thinks they know more about *who* you are than *you* do.

Yes. *You* are the creator of your self-esteem.

And only *you* can open the door.

Learning 42

I REJECT THE IDEA THAT LIFE NEEDS TO BE HARD

'Being effortless is the coolest thing in the world.'

STELLA MCCARTNEY

Work *hard*. Strive *hard*. Live *hard*.

This is the message we're fed, even in our primary-school years, as we grow and lose the innocence, acceptance and ease of childhood.

How we think as adults is significantly different from how we thought when we were young. Somewhere along the line, as we emerged from childhood, we began to hear from others that 'life is hard'; that we must struggle to achieve whatever it is that we want; that nothing worth having comes easily. Sound familiar? Maybe you've heard these words come out of your own mouth. I know I have, in my less aware moments.

Such messages are unhelpful and misleading because they transport our thoughts and our efforts and source them in fear and self-doubt.

If it's all so hard, what's going to make *us* so brilliant that we'll be able to rise to the challenge and succeed?

Our minds become negative, anxious and scared, and they have the power to maroon us in a place we don't actually want to be, but where we remain because we are so afraid of leaving it and failing.

When I finished writing *The New Mum's Notebook*, I was uncharacteristically lacking in self-doubt and I didn't question my achievement. It hadn't been hard: it had seemed effortless. I still feel as though it wrote itself (which, of course, it did). As I was waiting for the self-published copies to arrive, however, there was a part of me that did start wondering whether it was going to be worth anything. After all, I hadn't put enough work or agony into it, had I? My mind had started generating those habitual thoughts again: *Nothing worth having comes easily.* Yet *The New Mum's Notebook* has reached places and countries my anxious mind could never have envisaged.

This taught me the lesson that, actually, life is only as hard as we make it. All my striving thus far hadn't actually got me anywhere. Yet, when I simply allowed and *did*, amazing things happened.

My separation further endorsed this. Something that was supposed to be so tragic and difficult has actually only freed me and allowed me to live my life with ease.

Now I reject the idea that life needs to be hard. It's only our thinking that makes it so.

Work *easily*. Strive *easily*. Live *easily*.

How much better does that sound?

Learning 43

I IGNORE THE IDEALS OF SOCIETY

'Our modern society is engaged in polishing and decorating the cage in which man is kept imprisoned.'

SWAMI NIRMALANANDA

There are messages all around us, infiltrating our consciousness every single day. We don't ask them in. They're just there. Cold-callers, intruding upon our thoughts.

Some of these messages are about relationships.

Because society likes us to be part of a pair. It favours couples and families with two parents of opposite sex. It is conservative in its origins. And, despite the fact that we are gradually starting to break out of these rigid constraints with developments such as same-sex marriage and parenting, society is still operating very much within them. For some people, it is still unimaginable for anyone to *choose* to be alone or to be able to thrive in a one-parent family.

Yet many do and many can. I do. And you can.

At the point of my separation, I made a choice to ignore society's ideals. As a single parent, I knew that I was entering a minority group that is often stereotyped and marginalized by society. And yet I didn't feel pitiable or down on my luck. Quite the opposite. I saw how fortunate I was to have another chance. I felt liberated from many of the issues still affecting so many of my peers.

Aside from my three children, I only have myself to think of. I am learning to rely on myself for my happiness, because I am accepting – through all the emotions and experiences of the past few years – that I am all I need.

If, one day, I become part of a 'pair' again, it will be through choice and personal desire, not because I need someone or because society will find me more acceptable as half of a couple.

On tricky days, those uninvited cold-callers are much more likely to play havoc with your thoughts and it can be harder to ignore the ideals of society. *If only* you were in a couple, *if only* you were parenting with the mother or father of your child(ren), everything would feel *right*.

But would it, really?

When you reach this point, just take a moment and ask yourself: is this *your* thought? Or do you just want to fit in? Think back and remember a moment when your solo status liberated and empowered you. That time you went to a party alone, for example, and had an amazing time because you didn't have someone else to chaperone.

The time you took all your children swimming, navigating the clammy changing rooms and damp clothing with just one pair of hands. The time you ate what *you* wanted to eat for dinner while watching trashy TV that would have numbed and irritated your ex-partner. Tap into that memory and remember that feeling of liberation.

Then think of someone else who inspires you because they also live 'outside' of society's expectations.

And free yourself, as you do time and time again.

Learning 44

I AM NOT FAZED BY THINGS I CANNOT CHANGE

'Do not allow the actions of others to decrease your good manners, because you represent yourself, not others.'

BUDDHA

I have spent a lot of time and energy questioning or trying to change outcomes that I cannot alter, because they are not *mine* to change.

So, now, I have stopped trying. This has resulted, very naturally, in me becoming unfazed by *that which I cannot change* – which is actually quite a lot.

This is a state that brings instant calm and peace. If I can't change it, then why am I expending precious energy on it? End of debate. That possibly sounds simplistic and impossible. But allow me to explain.

When I look at what I can change this very minute, I see my mood, my energy, my momentum, the attention I give to my thoughts, how I choose to see something and how I speak or behave towards someone else.

When I consider what I *can't* change, I see someone *else's* mood, energy, momentum, attention, thoughts, how *they* choose to see something and how *they* speak or behave towards me or someone else. It's what we talked about in Learning 38 and it's a theme that runs throughout this book – *us* not *them*.

Do not underestimate the power of your words and thoughts in what you end up creating. Whenever I've allowed myself to perpetuate a low victim vibration, spoken negative words and expletives, or even spoken poorly of another, guess what I've attracted? More and more of the same, plunging me deeper into the abyss. When I've seen that I can't change something but I *can* change how I react to it, my subsequent experiences have been easy and pleasurable. I become unfazed.

Consider it. What *can* you change? What *can't* you change?

In the realm of separation, *knowing* we don't *have* to be fazed means that any reaction we have to our ex-partner's actions can be diffused by just reminding ourselves that we cannot change *their* behaviour. Just as it isn't possible for us to know their true motivation (see Learning 28), it isn't possible for us to *change* their actions.

We can change our response, however, and that *may* influence the outcome. It will certainly change *our* experience into a more pleasurable one.

Ultimately, the outcome is the outcome. And we must allow it, whatever *it* is.

That acceptance always restores a level of peace.

It is what it is.

Learning 45
I ATTRACT MY OUTCOMES

'Expect something good to happen to you no matter what happened yesterday.... Let the past go. A simply abundant world awaits.'

SARAH BAN BREATHNACH, *SIMPLE ABUNDANCE*

While someone else's outcome may not be our business or responsibility, our own is completely within our control.

Why not attract the best one we can?

I know now that I attract my outcomes mostly through mood, thought, momentum and action. Or a combination of all four.

I think myself into attraction. Or I feel myself. Or, sometimes, I have to *do* something in order to shift my momentum. Running usually does it for me, and every now and again I do some meditation, on my own terms – it's nowhere near as intimidating as I once imagined it to be. I just have to figure out what will work for me, in that moment. And get on with it. You can do the same.

When attraction is flowing with ease and love, it feels easy to draw in more. That was my whole experience of my first year of separation. But when we're in a challenging or uncomfortable place and our energy is stuck, it feels *far* more difficult.

So as we learn to live more consistently in alignment with ourselves and are more aware of just how much influence we can have over what happens next – for *us*, not someone else – we can shift this momentum more rapidly (more about this in Learning 52).

When you simply *can't* shift the thoughts, I recommend taking action, doing something – anything – for 10 minutes (see Learning 19). Exercise is particularly effective because moving the body and focusing your mind on your physical being and breathing takes it away from your thoughts. Exercise *feels* good (even the painful parts) and it reminds you that you are something *other* than your mood and thoughts and *you* can override them.

On the first day of my period, for example, I often feel lethargic. One month, I woke up feeling extreme lethargy. I had the luxury of a day without my children and yet I felt completely unmotivated, despite having a list of chores and some lovely things to do that I knew would ultimately lift me.

But I couldn't get out of bed, even to make a coffee.

Then, just like that, I realized I *could* attract a different outcome. I didn't have to spend the day feeling despondent and crampy, just because that's what day one of my period is *usually* like.

So I got up.

I did just 15 minutes of HIIT on my bedroom floor.

I made a coffee.

And, one by one, I did all my chores, didn't give my period a second thought and had a really satisfying day.

It took me two years to reach this magical place, where *I* could determine the day ahead of me. All those moments of focusing on 'the next 10 minutes' – and all the mini outcomes that have resulted and fed into the next one – have shown me that I *can* and I *do* attract my own outcome. My own series of outcomes. Every single time.

The ultimate outcome being that I am now mostly able to align myself on the tougher days as easily as I can on the easier days. It's complete empowerment and it changes your life and what you can achieve.

So go ahead and attract what *you* deserve. Think. Feel. Channel. Do.

And, if you haven't yet had the experiences – the practice – to know that you attract your own outcomes, I hope this shows you that you *can*.

And you *will*.

Learning 46
I ALLOW MYSELF TO TRUST

'When you run into these issues where fear has such a dominant place, you're either going to go to control or you're going to go to trust.'

WILLIAM PAUL YOUNG, SUPER SOUL PODCAST

How many of us trust, absolutely and without exception, as we say that we do?

The nature of trusting – in yourself, your situation and others – is unconditional. Otherwise, surely, it's something else? This means that we must retain that firm belief, even when it feels shaky; *especially* when it feels shaky.

When everything around us seems to be falling down, we need to allow ourselves to fall with it, safe in the trust that when we land, while our bones may be broken, our hearts will already be healing.

But how do we allow ourselves to trust, *no matter what?*

We rise above the fear that is causing us to doubt and react and we choose to trust in ourselves and/or another, regardless of the situation that confronts us.

Simply put, we *allow* it.

We know that control, as a default, is no good for us, so that leaves trust as the only option.

We *allow* it.

I feel that this is a good place to address the desire to have children because, if it seems as though the very possibility of ever becoming a parent is being threatened by the end of your relationship, you need to head towards trust. Through the learnings so far, you are beginning to see that you can make your own rules and attract your own outcomes; becoming a parent is no exception to this and no one's journey into parenthood is the same. Behind every life shared by a parent and child is a melting pot of scenarios: intentional, surprising, conventional, extraordinary – all united by taking a giant leap of faith. Allow yourself to trust that *your* child is coming.

Learning to trust in ourselves unconditionally is one thing, but *can* we really trust in others, no matter what? Your relationship may already have suggested that you can't, if your partner was unfaithful or deceitful in some way.

So let's talk about the couple who have experienced infidelity. We naturally talk about trust in this scenario; they go hand in hand because the trust has been 'broken' and it will take time to rebuild, if it can even *be* rebuilt. Yet there are couples who, before they even start this journey, know without doubt that they will get through it. They trust in *something* – themselves as individuals, their relationship, their love – to *allow* them to go on and process the hurt. That trust never waivers. This is not to say that the people who *do* separate as a result of infidelity are doomed. Far from it! Many will go on to trust another partner and have a fulfilling relationship despite their previous experience, because their instinct to trust in this new offering of love is greater than their fear.

Then there is the relationship between parent and child. If my eldest daughter lies to me, I feel that she is threatening my trust, just by the very act of doing so. But if I look at it in another way – a trusting way – I instead *trust* that there is a reason *why* she is lying to me – probably fear – and I enable that fear to be alleviated for her, so that she can share the truth with me. I retain my firm belief in *her* and she retains hers in me.

Isn't that what trust has to be? Unconditional. Unwavering. Safe.

I see now that a lack of trust – in ourselves and also in others – is rooted in *our own personal fear*; something that threatens our equilibrium. And that, faced with this fear, we choose control and action when we should simply lean back.

Allow yourself to trust. *No matter what.* Even if that takes you to an uncertain place. Even if that means putting your trust in someone who has 'let you down'. Even if that means trusting in the outcome of a different, seemingly less favourable situation, such as separation, bankruptcy or whatever it may be.

Especially then.

Learning 47

I AM MY VERSION
OF SUCCESSFUL

*'Most of us assume that success leads to happiness...
once we get the dream job, home or partner, life will
feel clicked into place. New research shows that if you
want success, you should first aim to be happy.*

James Wallman, *Time and How to Spend It*

When we say, 'I want to be successful,' it's a bit like when we say, 'I just want to be happy.' We probably haven't stopped to figure out what either success or happiness look like to us. Although it probably does include the dream job, home and partner.

But *success* is just a word. And, on its own, it doesn't mean very much.

In our society, success and even happiness is usually defined by status, wealth and comparison; how *our* lives compare in relation to others.

I know that after separation success feels out of reach for many, who see the end of their relationship as a great and shameful failure on their part.

But success is so much more than the weak and limited definition our society has created. Knowing what I know now, I would say that success is simply *living your life in alignment with you*, whatever other 'riches' this does or doesn't bring.

Over the past few years I have had much insight into the emptiness of the traditional interpretation of success – relationships *and* career – and I have come to the realization that success is *only* meaningful if it meets *my* criteria; not someone else's.

In a world where everyone is *striving* for success, recognition and validation – and where it seems more accessible for *everyone* – it's easy for *your* version to be diminished.

But every journey each of us takes follows our own unique path. The true merit of everything in our lives is how authentically it fulfils what we are trying to create. My success will *always* look different to someone else's version of it. And so will yours.

That realization brings humility and gratitude. As well as relief. Because once you are aware, you'll be less likely to be drawn into those misperceptions again.

So, while the end of my marriage may understandably appear as failure to others, I can only see the success of my separation and all the wonderful things it continues to show me. It has given me cause to ask myself the big questions: what do I enjoy doing?; how do I want to spend my time, my work, my life? It has given me the opportunity to have so many new experiences that have helped me feel successful in new, simpler terms and in the smallest of ways.

Now, success looks like whatever I want it to look like: it's practising spellings with my daughter before school; writing a chapter of my latest book; being motivated enough to throw some random ingredients into the slow cooker; or taking my kids backpacking.

And I have *never* felt as 'successful' as I do now because, finally, I know how to live my life in alignment with *me*.

Learning 48

I FEEL THINGS I'D SOMETIMES RATHER NOT

'Feelings are just visitors. Let them come and go.'

MOOJI

It reassures me when I hear that people who live their lives more meaningfully, spiritually or in awareness than me still wobble, sometimes.

To be human is to be uncertain and vulnerable. So it makes complete sense that we will not always feel the way we would like to feel, even when we have been practising it so diligently.

Anger. Envy. Resentment. None of these are emotions we aspire to. But they will happen, regardless of our desire for them and, if we let them take hold, we will only attract more of that energy.

I mentioned the importance of accepting *all* of our emotions in Learning 7 and I'm reintroducing it in this section because it is important that we actually feel *comfortable* with this reality. That we understand 'negative' emotions will arise – even when we've been flying high for a while, even when we've been living a life of awareness for some time. Otherwise, we are likely to continue to berate ourselves whenever we feel this way, because we believe it should be different by now. *We* should be different.

We're doing amazingly. As we are.

When we feel these emotions, we're likely to resume the bad habit of evaluating ourselves and our lives according to the definitions of others. That old enemy of alignment again: comparison (see Learning 47).

Well, not that I wish to encourage you and not that it matters, but I'll just remind you that every now and again *everyone* feels like this. *Everyone.*

You may feel anger that your ex-partner seems to have moved on more quickly than you. Or envy that your friend has *everything* you thought you would have. Perhaps it's resentment because your dreams of a loving relationship, children or financial security now seem way above the clouds, out of reach.

You don't want to feel this way, and you won't – not for very long (or ultimately). But telling yourself *not* to feel isn't an effective option and it won't ease the discomfort.

And, in the meantime, allow. Don't judge. Let it pass. Choose to use kind, uplifting words and be aware of the ones you utter that judge and chastise. You'll never feel better for speaking them out loud or for joining in someone else's rant session.

Do something to attract the feelings you'd prefer to be experiencing.

You're doing amazingly. As you are.

Learning 49
I TRANSFORM GUILT INTO LOVE

'Guilt is the teacher, love is the lesson.'
JOAN BORYSENKO

I have long believed that guilt is an expression of love.

After all, we feel guilt mainly when we've acted out of alignment or when we feel ashamed of something we'd rather not have done. Our true self knows we have drifted away momentarily, and that makes us experience the emotion we've labelled as guilt. In that moment, we want to have been kinder, calmer, more compassionate.

All states that are sourced in love.

When it comes from within us and isn't inflicted upon us by another person or an external source, guilt is a useful prompt to move us back into alignment with our loving self.

Guilt is the desire to return to love.

So if you've treated yourself or someone disrespectfully, lost your temper at your ex, shouted at your children because you're tired or jumped the gun and not taken the time to understand another perspective, don't dwell on feelings of guilt. Instead, *use* them to identify which behaviour you'll change so that, next time, you can act from a place of love.

If the guilt is inflicted upon us by another, it is never *our* remorse to start with; don't waste your energy trying to process guilt imposed by someone else.

And, finally, guilt is a state we can learn not to engage with, if we remember that nothing is ever *wrong* anyway – it's only wrong to think we are.

Learning 50
I AM
EMOTIONALLY AWARE

*'How you authentically feel in any given moment
is not necessarily who you authentically are.'*
MARIANNE WILLIAMSON, SUPER SOUL PODCAST

I have always been emotionally charged.

Now, however, I can see that being emotional and being emotionally aware are not the same. The former is how we feel, although we don't always know why; the latter is being aware of where that emotion originates from and how we deal with it.

When my emotion has come from love, it has mostly served me well; when it has originated from fear, not so much. There have been *many* times when I simply should have walked away but I was unable to because I wasn't able to pinpoint the real source of my emotional rush and manage my response accordingly.

A little while ago, however, I *allowed* someone to speak badly to me and, even though it was completely undeserved and unprompted, I didn't try to correct them. When I got home I cried, but my friend pointed out that what I had failed to do was notice how amazing my calm response had actually been. My habitual self was telling my inner self that I should have fought back, hence my strong emotional response. But, of course, we should never respond to rudeness with rudeness, because then we are not being our true, loving selves. And that person's rudeness was never about me in the first place; it was a complete lack of emotional awareness on their part.

I, on the other hand, had started my journey of emotional awareness and had walked away.

Separation has allowed me to practise this *a lot*. I have seen how many of the interactions between me and my ex-husband stem from fear and a desire to control, on both our parts. I have learned to lean back from my fearful emotions 80 per cent of the time. Because that emotion, no matter how real or authentic it feels while I'm experiencing it, is *not* actually me.

Now, when I feel a strong emotion rising, I always see it as a sign, a trigger to notice something that needs my attention. I try to sit with it for a moment so I can understand it. Sometimes this feels incredibly uncomfortable and I would much prefer to drown it out by responding with an angry text, having a glass of wine or doing something else to sate the emotional rush. But, as I have learned, emotions that arise from fear – envy, anger, anxiety, hatred – always need to be *felt* in order for them to pass. This doesn't mean you always have to engage with them – quite the opposite, in fact, because acting upon feelings that hurt *you* will only ever produce destructive consequences. But it does help when you know *where* those feelings are coming from.

When I can't lean back effectively – it's especially hard if I'm tired, stretched or hormonal – and something happens that overwhelms me with emotions, resulting in me reacting in a way I'd rather I hadn't, I reflect afterwards – not as an opportunity to berate myself, but to find the learning in that situation.

What did the universe want me to notice in the calmer moments that followed, after I lost my temper? There is always something, even if that was only another chance to see how I could react differently in future.

That is being emotionally aware and it gets easier the more we do it.

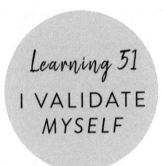

Learning 51
I VALIDATE MYSELF

'Stop looking outside for scraps of pleasure or fulfilment, for validation, security or love – you have a treasure within that is infinitely greater than anything the world can offer.'

ECKHART TOLLE, *THE POWER OF NOW*

I am the only person who can define my own intentions, truth and substance. No one else. Only me.

Separation forces us to stand alone, to feel the unique ground beneath us, to define ourselves *as* ourselves. For many of us, separation will be the first time that we have visited this experience in some time – possibly ever.

Once I started to validate myself, I realized how foolish it was to expect anyone else to do this for me. A partner. A friend. A work colleague. A social media acquaintance.

Insecurity is a conduit for giving impetus to what someone else thinks of you. And it's irrelevant. Your existence is valid simply because you are here, right now, learning to fulfil your unique purpose (see Learning 97).

Of course, at times we all *appreciate* some validation – that's the very nature of that bond we feel when we read or hear something that resonates with our own thinking. But that feeling is more about human connection and shared experience than the need for something to be true in order for *us* to believe it about ourselves.

Relinquishing the desire for others to validate you allows you to really connect with *yourself*, without external influences or pressures. You go into your purpose, with ease and without conflict.

You know who *you* are and what *you* desire. And so you attract the perfectly aligned outcome.

The one that is waiting only for *you*.

Learning 52

I COME
BACK QUICKLY

'Sometimes life is going to hit you in the
head with a brick. Don't lose faith.'

STEVE JOBS

We all crash; even the most successful entrepreneurs and thought-leaders in life. *Especially* those, in fact.

It never matters *that* we crash. All that matters is how quickly it takes us to come back.

Since childhood, I have always crashed hard and outwardly. It's the very process of learning that emotional awareness we've just talked about.

But I would find it difficult to get out from under the rubble, and I would also feel ashamed that I had ever felt or acted that way in the first place – the peril of sharing emotions and woes so publicly.

A couple of weeks after I *thought* my ex-husband and I were finally moving forwards in our separation, we hit another roadblock.

The fallout, for me, was massive. I felt it in every bone and muscle of my body. I couldn't catch my breath and the lethargy was overpowering. I dropped the kids at school, cried, watched a bad movie on TV, cried some more, went to bed, then cried until it was time to pick the kids up, when I dragged myself to school, collected the kids and promptly went back to bed.

I lay. I slept. I lay. I slept. My eldest daughter brought me some Marmite pasta that she'd cooked for herself, her sister and her brother to eat for dinner.

A couple of hours later, as it fell dark outside, I woke up to my four-year-old kissing me. The combination of rest – mental and physical – and the purity of his little joyous, innocent face in that very moment healed me. The lethargy shifted.

So I got up.

And, while it was an intense crash, it was a quick one.

Because I had allowed it. I had listened to my body and let my mind close down.

And then I came back.

So allow yourself the fallout and don't feel any shame for having it. Do it privately, do it publicly, but *however* you do it, know that what awaits you at the end is a little more healing, a little more clarity and another experience that, once again, highlights how strong you are. And subsequent fallouts – though I hope they will be few and far between – are never to be feared because they serve to remind you that you *always* come back.

Learning 53
I FIND
MY OWN WAY

'To find your own way is to follow your bliss.'

JOSEPH CAMPBELL, *THE POWER OF MYTH*

I have never really liked asking for directions. I don't always use my GPS (or even trust it when I do). My kids often joke when we're on the way to a party, 'Do you actually *know* the way this time, Mum?'

It wasn't until I sat down to write this chapter that I'd ever given this much thought. Then I realized: *I like to find my own way.*

And I do, I *really* do. Someone else telling me where to go and how to get there is like knowing the end of a book before I begin reading it. It spoils it. Where is the instinct, the excitement and the journey, if someone else does it for you?

Historically, I've always ended up getting *somewhere*, even if, as with separation, it wasn't the metaphorical destination I'd planned or expected. So often that destination has turned out to be more illuminating and fulfilling than the one I'd originally set out to reach.

The wonderful summer when the kids and I spent a week driving around the east of the UK in a camper van illustrates this point well. I had made a few plans but I soon realized that the fun and liberation of such a trip lay in finding our own way and getting off the beaten track; so much so that one night we even abandoned a campsite to camp wild on the beach – an experience that will stay with me forever. After waking up at 6:30 a.m. to the sound of the lapping waves, I had a freezing and invigorating early-morning swim in the sea before making bacon sandwiches on our gas hob and feeling my heart burst as I watched my four- and six-year-old wash up together on the pebbles.

Then there was the summer when we backpacked our way along the Turquoise Coast of Turkey, without *really* knowing how to get from place to place until the time came to just find our way.

Both of these trips were literal examples of how much I have changed during the course of separation; of everything separation has given me so far. Independence. Spontaneity. Faith.

Ironically, I think my ex-husband would rather like the spontaneous, adventurous person I've become.

These trips have been the best thing my kids and I have ever done together. That *I* have ever done.

And I know unequivocally that, literally or metaphorically, I am *always* going to find my own way.

Without ever needing to know the destination.

PART 5

UNIQUENESS

ALLOWING YOURSELF TO
APPRECIATE *YOURSELF*

Wonderful you.

Halfway through this book and this journey, it's now time for you to start to really appreciate *you*.

We don't do this often enough. It feels alien. Uncomfortable. Perhaps a bit narcissistic. We focus on our weaknesses and lose sight of our strengths. If you find it difficult to accept a compliment, this part is especially for you.

I hope that separation is already showing you just how unique you are. We may all approach it differently but we certainly do it with similar strength.

You are unique.

And it's really important that you start to notice yourself in this way. It might take a little prompting initially, so here are 11 learnings that helped me do just that.

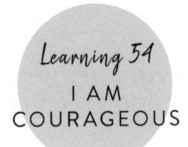

Learning 54

I AM
COURAGEOUS

'Courage starts with showing up and letting ourselves be seen.'
BRENÉ BROWN, *DARING GREATLY*

Those of us who are going through a separation probably don't consider ourselves to be courageous. Probably not until someone else points it out are we likely to consider applying the term to ourselves.

But separation, however it happens, makes you brave. There is no doubt.

It takes you from a place of great vulnerability to one of great courage. It makes you question the order of things. It allows you to get to know yourself. It encourages you to break free from routines you'd become a slave to and try new things. 'Why not?' becomes your mantra.

You have nothing to lose; you have already shown yourself that through loss you can also gain so much. You are becoming more comfortable 'not knowing', which in turn unleashes a new sense of adventure.

Choosing or accepting to go it alone *is* brave and is not something everyone would do. So when the days are tricky, you've lost your way or you're feeling desperate to know what your future holds, please remind yourself of this. Say the words out loud: 'I am courageous.' And then tell yourself that again as many times as you need to until you believe it.

The truth is that navigating separation will probably make you so brave that nothing will faze you again in quite the same way. You will engage with fear far less than you once did because you have faced the unknown and thrived.

You are that tower of resilience. And you keep on getting taller and taller.

Learning 55
I AM GRACEFUL

'The trick is to be grateful when your mood
is high and graceful when it is low.'
RICHARD CARLSON, DON'T SWEAT THE SMALL STUFF

Have you ever noticed how graceful people seem to float around effortlessly and without ever encountering conflict?

I used to think grace was an inherent quality, but grace can actually be learned and practised, much like any behaviour. And, like anything else, the more you seek it out, the more natural it becomes.

When graceful people are late, you'd never know. When they're struggling, they remain calm. They respect themselves deeply and also respect those around them.

Choosing grace during a separation has a transformative effect. It stops you reacting from a place of tension or discontent so you can avoid perpetuating the cycle of dispute.

It helps you to form intentions that will serve you well, long into your future, such as never speaking badly of your ex-partner in public or over the internet. I have always held strong to this intention. While there have of course been times when I have felt injustice in my situation, I have only ever shared my feelings privately with my family or a close friend who understands (I engage with the 'injustice' infrequently these days). Ranting on social media and trying to create 'sides' will never make you feel better. And there *will* come a day when it won't all feel quite so raw. You'll make your peace with whatever has happened and, when you do, you'll be so glad you didn't tell anyone and everyone who would listen how awful your ex-partner was. Remember, what anyone else *thinks* they know about what happened means nothing: know your truth (see Learning 38).

Furthermore, shining your kindness inside and out will remind the other person of who you *really* are. Of the person with whom they fell in love in the first place. That in itself has a powerful healing effect for you, because it keeps you in alignment with yourself and it lessens that likelihood of being misinterpreted or misunderstood.

Being graceful is *not* about being closed or pretending that life is perfect. It's simply about making a choice to handle situations in a way that doesn't make *you* feel uncomfortable or inauthentic afterwards.

It's the ultimate gift of kindness to yourself.

It's grace.

Learning 56
I AM GRATEFUL

*'I am fortunate to be alive. I have a precious
human life. I am not going to waste it.'*
DALAI LAMA, FROM *THE BOOK OF JOY*

I am not owed anything. And neither are you.

That statement will either have you nodding in agreement or
maybe it will make you feel indignant. You *are* owed. You're owed the
relationship you thought you were going to have. You're owed
the respect of your ex-partner. You're owed the life you were
living.

You may have deserved it, of course. But debt and reward are not the
same thing and they don't operate in the same way.

I spent more time than I probably even realize feeling that my
ex-husband *owed* me. I felt he owed me for the years that we'd lost
and particularly for the 'special new baby times' and the subsequent

family years I would possibly now never experience with a loving, compatible partner.

And yet, as the separation has progressed, I have learned that I was not *entitled* to all of these things. They were never guaranteed. I sowed my choices and I reaped their consequences. My ex-husband owes me nothing.

Instead, I see that I have so much to be grateful for. And I am.

I am owed *nothing* because I have *everything*, as long as I don't expect *my* everything to look exactly like someone else's.

I expect nothing from my life now, going forwards. I'll continue to sow, reap and learn, along the way.

And be grateful for every crop I harvest.

Learning 37
I CHALLENGE OTHERS

"Normality is a paved road: it is comfortable to walk upon, but no flowers grow there."

VINCENT VAN GOGH

Not everyone will find your separation easy or positive.

Aside from very normal issues, like people not knowing what to say or mutual friends being unsure how to socialize with you both, there are other factors that mean friends or acquaintances may fall away. It's not personal and it's rarely about you.

Some people will just prefer you as part of a couple. They know which box to put you in so that you don't challenge the equilibrium of their world.

For others, your separation, especially if it was your choice, may bring up uncomfortable feelings about their own relationship or marriage – feelings that they have been suppressing and still aren't ready to face, or might never be.

Your very presence may be challenging to them, not only through your separation from your partner but in everything 'new' that you subsequently do. You'll certainly intrigue them. For some, seeing you and your partner splitting up can trigger their own insecurities and fears: *'What if this happens to me?'* Some people would just rather not be around that reality for fear of somehow inviting it in. 'It's not catching,' as I say to others, even though several of my friends have actually since gone through separation themselves.

Before my own separation, I remember feeling a pang of envy when I heard of others separating or starting again. I wondered how they were brave enough. At that point, realizing that my marriage was not what I wanted it to be, I felt trapped. How would I ever leave when things weren't actually bad enough to force me to go?

And this is what some will tell you: 'Everyone feels like this after years together. It's normal.' I was even asked, 'Why do *you* deserve more?'

I have since learned that no, not everyone *does* feel like that and no, we don't have to accept it as 'normal'. Some couples are truly happy and compatible and, despite the difficult times, they grow together and end up stronger than they were in the beginning, which is how all relationships should progress. In mutual growth.

So yes, I *do* deserve more.

So does my ex-husband.

And so do *you*.

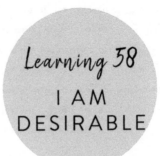

Learning 58

I AM DESIRABLE

'Form a habit of finding yourself beautiful.'

REGENA THOMASHAUER,
MAMA GENA'S SCHOOL OF WOMANLY ARTS

One of the things on which separation impacts considerably is your ability to believe that you are still desirable, not just physically but also emotionally and intellectually.

In the end, you and your partner possibly failed to even notice one another, least of all compliment one another, celebrate each other's achievements or share any degree of intimacy.

But do we have to be *desired* to be desirable? Are we only desirable if someone else tells us we are? Is it possible to find *ourselves* desirable? Or is that the very definition of narcissism?

The Law of Attraction would say that in order to be desired by another, we would first have to desire *ourselves*. Like attracts like. How can we expect someone else to be drawn to us in that way if we are not drawn to ourselves?

At the point at which my ex-husband and I separated, it was my general opinion that I must not be a very attractive person. I hadn't 'let myself go' during our marriage or post-children, but how could I be considered attractive under the circumstances?

It took me some time to rebuild my self-esteem and to truly believe that not being desirable to *him* did not mean that I was not desirable, full stop. Once I had understood this, I started to make more of an effort. I exercised even more because it made me feel good. I chose something out of the wardrobe instead of defaulting to the old faithful jeans that lived on the blanket box at the bottom of the bed; it only took a couple of minutes longer each morning and it lifted my spirits.

In his absence, I realized that I felt so much more desirable than I had *ever* done even when my ex-husband had been there. And it meant I wasn't irritated by someone failing to notice when I *had* made an effort, either. I learned to admire myself.

I wasn't doing any of this to attract someone else. I did it entirely for myself, very instinctively. I wanted to feel good not just on the outside but, more importantly, on the *inside*. Desirability is such an intrinsic combination of the physical and mental.

And that is how I discovered that desirability is no different to everything else we experience.

It begins and ends with us.

Learning 59

I EMPOWER MYSELF

'Put your future in good hands. Your own.'
MARK VICTOR HANSEN, *CHICKEN SOUP FOR THE SOUL*

The feeling of empowerment comes and goes in life and in separation, but it *is* something we can summon. Once we know this, it is our greatest ally in moving forwards.

You have been learning to empower yourself since the beginning of this separation journey and I hope you're managing it, at least some of the time.

On days when you're feeling disempowered and you need to dig a little deeper, it can be helpful to remind yourself of the benefits that come from empowerment:

~ Not being a victim

~ Creating possibility

~   Taking responsibility

~   Leading by example

~   Inspiring others

~   Deciding your own path

~   Feeling joy

Presented with a list like this, you know that living in the alternative – a world in which you stay disempowered – is no longer an option. So, tell yourself how well you're doing and then keep going.

Separation, by definition, is the process of distinguishing between two or more things. In this case, distinguishing *you* from your partner; raising you up to be the empowering entity you have always had the ability to be – the only entity you *can* empower.

And this must remain your focus when the noise around you tries to distract you from your path. When your ex-partner makes a comment or performs an action that triggers you to react against your intention. When a friend unwittingly – or not – destabilizes your faith in yourself and your solo situation.

Anytime this happens to me – and it does, because we are all human beings with feelings – I lean back and take some time for myself, *with* myself, to reconnect with who I am becoming and where my path is leading me. In other words, I hold onto my power, instead of carelessly giving it away to words or actions that will only serve to disempower me.

Keep empowering *yourself.*

Learning 60
I AM
EMPATHETIC

*'Empathy is a quality of character that can change the world –
one that makes you understand that your obligations to others
extend beyond people who look like you and act like you...'*

BARACK OBAMA, COMMENCEMENT ADDRESS 2006,
UNIVERSITY OF MASSACHUSETTS AT BOSTON

Until something happens to rock our world, I think we can be resilient in an almost arrogant way. We feel invincible because we have no reason to believe otherwise.

However, once we've been through a major life event such as illness, an accident, losing a job, losing someone close, separation or even having a baby, afterwards and in time we are resilient in a compassionate way.

We understand humility. We project it. We seek to connect with others through our experiences and might even share our own to help others who are at the start of a similar journey. We take them with us and walk alongside them.

I empathize with others far more since I've had children, post-natal depression and gone through a separation. I have seen at first hand how delicate the human psyche is, but also how easily it can be empowered. And, while I know that we can absolutely do this on our own, it is a far more pleasurable existence doing it alongside others who understand and can co-create with us.

So I try to stay open and connect with *everyone* I encounter – a word of encouragement to the woman wrestling to get her toddler in his buggy, a smile for the driver who gesticulates at me because they're in a hurry, some chit-chat in the coffee queue – empathy matters, as we said in Learning 22. Trying to put ourselves in someone else's shoes – to see the world through their eyes for a moment – is a great exercise to remind us that *everyone* is going through *something*.

And that we *all* desire and deserve this human connection.

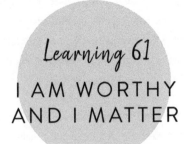

Learning 61
I AM WORTHY
AND I MATTER

'You yourself, as much as anybody in the entire universe, deserve your love and affection.'

<small>BUDDHA</small>

This is a mantra that is worth repeating to yourself daily: *I am worthy and I matter.*

In childhood and youth we own our self-worth, instinctively and exclusively – ironically when we're most likely to be perceived as selfish. As we grow, our self-worth becomes more dependent upon others. And when we enter a relationship, if we don't continue to own it, its existence can become completely defined by our partner, just like our desirability (see Learning 58).

Allowing someone else to define our worth and how much we matter means that our sense of self will always be reliant upon *them*, which is a situation that is only as sustainable as their perception of us.

In the case of separation, then, not very sustainable at all.

So how do we convince ourselves again that we do have worth?

The way we speak to ourselves – language and tone – and the 'story' we tell ourselves about *who we are* is crucial in rebuilding self-worth. Don't make it up. Dig deep for the truth. Find those nice words and praise yourself at least twice as much as you berate yourself (better still, don't berate yourself at all).

Since my separation, I have been making a conscious effort to raise my children *never* to have cause to doubt their self-worth. In becoming more aware of how I speak to *them*, I noticed in the process that often I didn't actually speak to myself very kindly. This was mostly born out of the fact that, in the last few years of marriage, my ex-husband and I were rarely kind to one another, verbally or otherwise. As a result, I had fallen out of practice at being kind.

Unsurprisingly, when you speak harshly or are unkind to others, you're damaging not only their self-worth but your own too, because you're moving further and further away from your true, loving self. It is very hard to believe 'I am worthy' if your actions and language imply the opposite.

When we focus on our self-worth, however, we naturally affirm the belief that we also *matter*, because we see ourselves independently of others and we trust in our own value, strength and purpose, which belong uniquely to us.

We are worthy and we matter.

Learning 62
I AM
UNIQUE

'I like me. And I like my story.'
MICHELLE OBAMA, SUPER SOUL PODCAST

I once wanted to be someone else. That *someone else* was always more measured, balanced and calm than me. More 'normal'. I imagined life would be *easier* if I was that type of personality.

Easier for whom, though? Easier for others who may have found me challenging, I suspect. Yet, as my friend says, we are *all* difficult to some.

I'm sure we've all dreamt of being someone else, even if the list of qualities in your imaginary persona are different from mine.

But. What an absolutely crazy thing it is to *wish* to be someone else. To not want to be you. Especially when someone else, right now, is possibly wishing *they* were you.

Looking back, I allowed my ex-husband to perpetuate my insecurities; he often labelled me as being highly strung, for example, as though it was an inherently negative quality, unable as he was to see or value the benefits such a trait also brought. I in turn failed to see the positives in his qualities too.

This is because, when we're in a bad relationship that isn't functioning, we no longer appreciate one another's unique qualities. The characteristics that probably attracted us to one another in the first place end up irritating us instead. Those strengths become flaws.

But each of us is so wonderfully unique, and we must always appreciate us *for ourselves*. No one will ever know you like *you* do (assuming you take the time to get to know yourself).

And, before you start labelling some of your qualities negatively, remember: we all have the qualities we're *meant* to have, in order to pursue our soul's purpose (more about this in Part 8).

Your purpose, which is *also* completely unique, to you.

So keep on being *you*.

(There's no one else worth being.)

Learning 63
I INSPIRE
OTHERS

'If life is a journey then let my soul travel and share your pain.'
SANTOSH KALWAR

Not many people know that they actually inspire others, just by being themselves, every day. It's hard to believe if you aren't doing something grand and 'impressive', such as curing cancer.

When others have told me that I've inspired them in some way – because I've shared my journey with depression or talked about my separation – it's felt slightly awkward to be praised for it. I was only doing something that came naturally to me and it helped me simultaneously to share.

Yet I also understand the sentiment. I've been on the receiving end of it when someone else has inspired me, endlessly. Because inspiring someone else is nothing grander than *enabling* them – to progress along their journey with a little more hope, joy and knowledge than they may otherwise have done without *you*.

The person who is newly separated, who sees through you that they are going to be just fine, too. The single parent who draws strength from the way *you* juggle your children, with ease and love. The separated person who hears *you* talk about separation from a place of possibility, not pity, and changes their mindset in the process.

If inspiring others is simply being open and willing to share our everyday lives alongside one another, then that is something we *all* have the capacity to do.

With hope and joy, not grandeur.

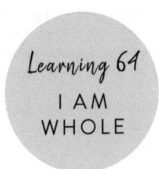

Learning 64
I AM
WHOLE

'She is a beautiful piece of broken pottery, put
back together by her own hands. And a critical
world judges her cracks while missing the beauty
of how she made herself whole again.'

J.M. STORM

I thought that in order to be *whole* you had to be that measured, balanced and calm person I mentioned in Learning 62.

Perfect. Smooth around the edges. No cracks.

But how can you possibly be whole if your experiences have fragmented you?

Now, I see that we are whole *because* of our cracks and all those experiences. Because it is those cracks that allow the light through to illuminate our souls, our inner beings and true selves.

So no, I am not whole in the *unbroken* sense. Because I have been broken many times. Many times, when separation has exhausted me and I can't find the energy to keep going, I have heard myself say those words: *I am broken.*

But I always put myself back together again. I am always my own glue. And while my edges may be a little rougher than before and while, over time, more cracks appear, they only serve to allow *more* light through. More illumination.

Never doubt your wholeness.

PART 6

INDEPENDENCE

RECOGNIZING YOUR ABILITY TO COPE AND THRIVE

I t is so important for you to see all that you hold down.

On the days where separation is an overwhelming proposition, it is healing to be able to acknowledge that you are doing so much better than you have otherwise convinced yourself.

On the days where separation *isn't* overwhelming, it is still a beautiful practice to praise and recognize yourself.

Did you even know you were so strong and capable? Did you ever suspect that you would thrive in such uncertain circumstances?

These next 11 learnings will illuminate some of the ways in which I've found myself to be capable and strong and they'll remind you to recognize your strengths, too.

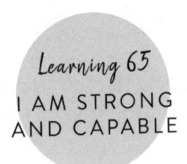

Learning 65
I AM STRONG
AND CAPABLE

'Physical strength in a woman – that's what I am.'

TINA TURNER

In the early months of separation, I realized how much I had become used to having someone by my side. To help me do 'stuff'. This was a rather surprising revelation because, in the latter years, I had convinced myself that my ex-husband never did anything at all on the domestic front.

But I obviously hadn't factored in the things he *did* do. Lighting the barbecue. Putting up the Christmas tree. Taking it down again and managing to remove it from the house without shedding all 13,243 pine needles. Building a fire. Helping with the practicalities of family holidays.

It's fair to say this doesn't sound very feminist of me. Despite being a woman who thought she was pretty independent, I had allowed him to do all these things simply because some of them were, to me, 'man tasks'.

Then, in the wake of separation, there was suddenly just me. Having to do it *all*, on my own.

And you know what? I've thrived.

I can now do a pretty decent barbecue (even if I did initially have to call a friend to talk me through it). My fires almost *never* go out. And as for taking out the first Christmas tree? Well, after shedding *all* its needles in the hallway, our bare tree got stuck in the doorway. While we did consider just leaving it there forever, with the help of all three kids we eventually got the carcass out – bald, but out.

The children and I have been on several holidays so far with me as a solo parent, including a UK camper van tour and a backpacking trip through Turkey. No one got lost and I even managed not to panic at my daughter's unexpected allergic reaction at Departures (probably the only scenario I *hadn't* imagined).

When my four-year-old left the tap running, I can proudly report that I unblocked the bathroom sink single-handedly, while also stopping the water that was pouring through the light fittings into the room below. My eldest wrote me the most wonderful note for that one:

> *You are so super, how did you do it? It was quite revolting when you got that gunk out. So I just wanted to say YOU'RE THE BEST!!! (at everything).*

Write a list – or even your own wonderful note to yourself – and I can guarantee you too will be amazed at how much you now do.

We have separation to thank for illuminating this strength and giving us the opportunity to discover and master new things.

It turns out that I am strong and capable.

And so are you.

(Just in case you were wondering.)

Learning 66

I CAN DEAL WITH
PROBLEMS QUIETLY

*'We cannot solve our problems with the same
thinking we used when we created them.'*
ALBERT EINSTEIN

I have always liked talking. My school report once read, 'Amy would
be a model student if she didn't talk quite so much.'

A fair point.

One of the fundamental ways in which my ex-husband and I were
mismatched, in fact, was in conversation. I liked to engage in it, often.
He thought words were superfluous beyond the basics of necessary
communication.

I wanted to talk everything through. Decisions. Problems. Life. It was
how I made sense of the world. Now, I do that through writing.

As our marriage progressed, I learned to talk these things through with friends and family instead, rather than risk the glazing over of his eyes.

So when we eventually separated, I was already used to doing a lot of the decision-making stuff alone. I didn't miss having his input on that side of things, as it had long since been extinguished.

What I did notice, however, was that the more time alone separation afforded me, the more I got used to being *quieter*. Quieter in my mind. Quieter in what I had to say. Quieter in asking for other people's advice. At the time, I wasn't sure if it was the result of pure exhaustion, looking after three kids on my own and an inability to process thoughts and speech, or due to something else.

I know now that it was the periods of solitude that allowed this quietness. Those periods are so important, yet so few of us actually get them.

Sometimes, I found myself simply putting a thought, problem or decision to one side, to deal with either later or not at all. It wasn't a form of denial; it was more a case of: 'I can't figure this out right now and I don't want to attract more energy to this issue by talking about it.'

You know the scenario. Something happens that you perceive to be awful. You talk it over with your friends. A sibling. The postman. Pretty much anyone who will listen. And before you know it, all you can think about is 'The Problem', which is now so big it has consumed every fibre of your being – and yet you are still no closer to resolving it.

Your best chance is to step back and quieten your mind.

While trusting that *being okay* is your ultimate truth.

(Because you always will be.)

Learning 67
I AM ALWAYS DOING MY BEST

'Your best is going to change from moment to moment...simply do your best, and you will avoid self-judgment, self-abuse, and regret.'
DON MIGUEL RUIZ, *THE FOUR AGREEMENTS*

Doing your best does not mean doing things flawlessly or impeccably *all* of the time. If you are acting in alignment with your values and intentions, *that* is your best. What else could it be?

It has taken me a long time to accept that I am *always* doing my best. I am doing my best when I perceive I do things 'well', but I am also doing my best when I perceive I don't, because those same values and intentions are mostly at the forefront of everything I do, even when I lose my way temporarily and have to realign myself afterwards.

In my separated situation, most of the time, I thrive. Some of the time, I cope. Occasionally, I falter. But: I am *always* doing my best, in every single one of these scenarios, and I accept that my best does not always look the same.

So when I lose my temper with the kids because I am tired, stretched or even hungry after feeding them several times and forgetting to eat myself, I am still doing my best. I am doing just as well then as I am when I sit calmly with them practising phonics or times tables.

It is my very best *in that moment* and it isn't for me to question my adequacy because there is no measure to gauge this; there are always variables.

We have actually always been doing our best, we just haven't had the self-awareness to acknowledge it.

Accept *your* best.

You're always doing it.

Learning 68
I AM
EXHAUSTED

'Once we accept our limits,
we go beyond them.'
ALBERT EINSTEIN

Exhaustion may not feel like a natural part of thriving; when our energy is depleted because we've taken on too much, we're 'failing' to do it all or we're near breaking point.

That doesn't sound much like thriving, does it?

Actually, however, exhaustion is a vital component of thriving; recognizing it is a huge strength (not a weakness) and we should be willing to declare it more often, on our own terms.

I am exhausted.

Acknowledging your own exhaustion is a positive step that enables you to step back, refocus (and reclaim) your energies in order to thrive once more. It is not dwelling on the exhaustion and thus attracting more; it's a process of recognition and re-evaluation.

Yet we don't always feel we have the right to do this, and so we perpetuate the state of exhaustion and hinder the reclamation of our energy.

Exhaustion, like so many things, has become a comparable condition. We measure it against others, against other people's situations, which *appear* more demanding and yet still they plough on. So we should be ploughing on. We feel guilty because, if they're pushing through their tiredness, surely we aren't entitled to feel that our tiredness is exceptional.

'*I'm exhausted.*'

'*I know, so am I.*'

No one wins in the tiredness stakes. No one is meant to. We are all allowed to be exhausted. We all have our own personal demands (see Learning 83). And we all have different levels of resilience at different points in our lives.

We are all different.

Separation with three children has unleashed a whole new level of exhaustion for me, but this does not mean that I am more entitled to feel it than, say, the happily married mum of two.

We are all different.

Exhaustion can actually be a highly satisfying state of being when it comes from acting on good energies. It's a different story when it comes from challenging times or sleepless nights, although there is still empowerment to be found simply in having seen those times through.

But we are doing ourselves a disservice if we pretend we aren't exhausted when we are. If we try to match someone else's 'strength'. If we power on through. If we don't operate on our own terms.

The person who recognizes their limits, refocuses their energies and replenishes their stores will be thriving again in no time.

Each of us can only do so much.

Each of us who recognizes this can go on to do so much more.

Learning 69
I TAKE CARE OF MYSELF

*'Taking care of yourself doesn't mean
me first, it means me too.'*
L.R. KNOST, *TWO THOUSAND KISSES A DAY*

There are so many human states in which, without consciously doing so, we can become martyrs in our own lives. We don't prioritize caring for *ourselves* because, on some level, we haven't deemed ourselves worthy of that care.

Remember: *I am worthy and I matter* (see Learning 61).

We cannot possibly thrive until we look after ourselves, mentally *and* physically. We will cope, and often well enough, but there is always fallout when we neglect ourselves.

Low vibrations, triggered when separation (and general life) makes us feel overwhelmed, are further aggravated by being tired, taking on too much, not exercising enough, eating badly, drinking without awareness, or coming down with illness. We need to give ourselves the *best* chance to thrive so we can move forwards with grace and purpose.

So, mostly, I try to eat well, go to bed before midnight, exercise and be aware of my thoughts and vibration. I don't always manage it, of course; there are so many curveballs in my life – in all of our lives – but I have learned that I cannot be reckless about taking care of myself. When I am, there is *always* fallout eventually. But when I care for myself, everything around me flows with ease.

Separation means that, aside from friends and family, there is only *you* to take care of you. This is an empowering realization, if you allow it to be, because it means you are about to prioritize yourself and commit to never neglecting yourself again.

Give yourself the best chance. Identify the things that are important to *you* in order to thrive and don't be reckless with them too often.

Because you are absolutely worthy of your own care.

Learning 70
I AM COMFORTABLE BEING ALONE

*'If one says: I cannot come because that is my hour
to be alone, one is considered rude, egotistical or
strange. What a commentary on our civilization,
when being alone is considered suspect.'*

ANNE MORROW LINDBERGH, *GIFT FROM THE SEA*

For some, being or spending time *alone* is undesirable, shameful and essentially an admission of being unpopular.

The more people we surround ourselves with, the more complete a person we must be. Because we are wanted and we belong. These are the rules of popularity; it needs other people for it to exist.

I've never done 'well' at trying to fit in or be at the top of everyone's invitation list and I've never made myself do things purely because I'm scared of missing out. That's an exhausting way to live.

I still have wonderful friends.

I never really understood why I was this way and I *have* in the past berated myself for not making more effort to be popular and follow the crowd. I know that, because of the way society works, there were opportunities that would have come to me had I been a 'social climber'. I also know that they'd have come at a price: my alignment and my authenticity.

Separation has shown me, through the enforced and regular periods of solitude it has given me, that I am just *really* happy being me and having any time alone. It's no more complicated than that.

At the very least, I have one day and one night a week where it is just me in my house. For 24 hours a week, I get to choose *how* I spend that time. It's indulgent. It's wonderful. It's gold dust, once you become a parent.

And I like spending time with myself. It's been one of separation's very generous gifts.

I choose *me*. I can be *selfish* – a word that needs defining more positively, because we should all regularly be more concerned with our own pleasure (see Learning 98).

And I am *absolutely* comfortable being alone.

Without suspicion.

Learning 71
I ENJOY
SLEEPING ALONE

'Sleep is the best meditation.'
DALAI LAMA

When I listen to others talking about their partner snoring or disturbing them at night, it makes me smile.

Because, four years in, I still love sleeping alone. Well, aside from the three small people who occasionally work their way under my duvet and sidle in beside me.

When I first separated, I still slept on my side of the bed. A force of habit. It was a while before I migrated into the middle, just because I could, and this is where I sleep now. I don't find it strange or lonely. It actually feels quite indulgent to climb into an empty bed with my book and hand cream.

I think it is really important – post-separation – to make your bedroom *yours*. Getting a new mattress is advised, if not a new bed frame too. A year in, I did both, as well as new pillows, duvet and linen. I should have done it sooner.

And it wasn't until recently that I had the sudden urge to move the furniture around. When I'd finished, I realized I had unintentionally removed all symmetry from the bedroom – the 'yours and mine' effect of having a bedside table each, and more. The energy in the room was immediately feminine and *all* mine.

It was a subconscious but powerful action. It freed another part of me. It moved me on another level. It made me engage with all the possibility of my future again.

Three days later, without any prior intent, I signed the divorce papers I'd been sitting on for weeks.

Learning 72
I AM
FINANCIALLY SECURE

'The opposite of more is enough.'
WILLIAM PAUL YOUNG, SUPER SOUL PODCAST

If you aren't entirely financially independent before separation – and so many of us aren't – the thought of going it alone is probably the biggest practical insecurity you'll face. Managing bills, dividing assets, learning to live on a lower budget, supporting children and possibly selling property; none of these feel comfortable, initially.

The chances are, most of us will *never* feel comfortable where money is concerned. I know people who have lots of it and yet still live with a perceived lack – 'I have no money' – because the lifestyle to which they have become accustomed takes all their income to maintain. They don't necessarily feel any more secure than the person who lives on minimum wage, striving to put food on the table for their family each week. They live in fear of losing it.

Financial security, like everything else, is a mindset. A story we tell ourselves. That's all.

Many of us don't even realize that we have a confused relationship with money, or that the relationship could be different. Instead, we live in *fear* of the money running out, the mortgage going up or losing our job. We live in *fear*.

Money has never made the world go round. It makes the world stand still. Because it roots us in that fear and stops us from fulfilling our purpose; from thinking it can be different.

But it *can* be different.

After all, no one wants money for money's own sake. If someone gives you one million pounds but you're not allowed to spend it, what use is that? Money is only the vehicle through which we acquire what we desire. And yet, so many of those things we desire aren't actual material things; they don't require money to be fulfilled. The extra money you tell yourself you need to buy *a bigger house* or get those *new trainers* you just must buy for your child because they really want them ('and all the other kids have them')? That isn't about money. There's a different intention beneath both of those material desires, surely?

That bigger house you want in order to have a spare room so friends can visit? That desire is really about spending more time with friends, and you can do that in other ways. Those trainers your child must have? That's about making your child happy – what every parent wants – but material goods have never made my kids as happy as they are when I just spend *actual* time with them, doing what they want (which usually costs nothing because they always make me play babies or pirates).

Money is just the vehicle we think we need to drive and, until we change our thinking, we'll always be running out of fuel.

My relationship with money used to be a fearful one. Every time I was on maternity leave, I worried about the money running out or about how we would make ends meet, even though fortunately we always did. As long as my attitude to money was fearful, I could never feel comfortable, no matter how much we did or didn't have.

I had an important lesson to learn there and the universe is still making sure I'm learning it now.

The day my ex-husband and I separated, I had no income of my own. This should have filled me with fear but it didn't. Instead, I believed in my financial security and the opportunity before me; I had self-published *The New Mum's Notebook* and 3000 copies of it had just arrived at my house. There was a very real chance that no one would buy it, but I had something to sell and I trusted they would. So I sold it, with conviction.

When I retell this anecdote, I notice that I always say, 'The timing was perfect.' Of course it was, because that is how I *chose* to see it.

Six months after self-publishing *The New Mum's Notebook*, I got a two-book deal and a modest advance. While I was thrilled, this actually took my thinking backwards, because it reignited that desire for financial security. That desire, as we've discussed, always becomes greater the more money you have and the more you see it dwindle away, as money always does.

As the hourglass ran out, I allowed myself to feel the fear, again.

I was confused by this fear and what it was telling me, because I didn't desire lots of money or lots of 'stuff' (at that point I hadn't bought a new pair of jeans in six years and didn't much care that my old ones had holes in). So what *did* I desire? I really just wanted to keep writing books. I wanted to do school drop-off and pick-up. I wanted to cook dinner for the kids each night.

These were my *intentions*. They had little to do with money: as long as I could find a way to have *enough*, I didn't need *more*.

So, as those grains of sand continued to trickle through the hourglass one by one, I decided to eliminate money from my thoughts. Because thinking in terms of lack always creates fear, and that fear gets in the way of our intentions. It mocks us and tells us we're not enough, we don't *have* enough and we can't really live our lives in *any* other way than that which we have been conditioned to do. Yet I'd already been living another way for the past few years.

As soon as I changed my focus, the answer came and, at 4:00 a.m. one morning, I saw how I could fulfil my intentions. I reduced my outgoings – how many non-essential things do we all pay for that we don't actually *have* to have to survive? – and I pitched for some writing jobs that were lower-paid than I was used to, but which would provide regular, reliable income and actually give me some new skills.

At that point I became financially secure. Secure in my thinking. Because I had found a viable way to secure my intentions.

It's always about the intentions.

Make sure you know what yours *really* are.

Learning 73
I AM DARING

*'There is freedom waiting for you, on the
breezes of the sky, and you ask, "What if I fail?"
Oh, but my darling, what if you fly?'*

ERIN HANSON

M y life is not 'safe', because I don't need it to be.

My life is not 'safe', because I don't want it to be.

My life is not 'safe', because I no longer *ask* for it to be.

Separation has allowed me to live outside the parameters of 'safety' in
every way possible, as shown in each learning I've shared in this book.
Because there is nothing I will do, from this point forwards, that will
feel more daring than the decision to leave my marriage.

It has unleashed endless possibility, opportunity and uncertainty.

Now, when I have an idea that won't leave my side, I pursue it. When I notice fear creeping in, I keep going. When others guide me towards 'safety', I remember that there is only uncertainty.

Daring, for me, isn't being reckless: I have three children to think about, although – being heavily outnumbered – I do have to take calculated risks sometimes. It isn't even jumping from a plane at great height (I did that once and probably won't again). It's more metaphorical than that: more about continuing to move away from habitual thinking – mine and others' – and about stepping out of the shadows that shroud me and into the exposure of light.

It's embracing every new experience that comes my way, not finding a thousand reasons to fold my arms and turn away in fear.

It's allowing myself to be vulnerable.

I am daring when my intuition calls for me to be; when the flutter in my heart and quickening of my pulse guides me more faithfully than my own habitual thinking or the opinions of other people.

I have no idea, mostly, how things will turn out, but that is the magic that keeps me going.

And sets me free, again and again.

Learning 74
I CAN
RAISE MY CHILDREN

*'Being a single parent is not a life full of
struggles, but a journey for the strong.'*
MEG LOWERY, FROM THE LIFE OF A SINGLE MOM WEBSITE

If your separation involves children, there will be days where the task
ahead of you seems gigantic and impossible.

I have found myself having such days many times and I continue to do
so. If this is you, too, it's okay.

Flying solo with kids in tow can, every now and then, feel overwhelming.
The sheer responsibility and juggling involved when you're a single
parent is challenging – being both parents so much of the time. There
will be times where you miss the shared responsibility of raising your
children. At bedtime, when bathing them and putting them to bed
feels like climbing a mountain. Or in the middle of the night, when
there is no one but you to deal with a wet bed, a nightmare, illness or
a restless sleeper.

We all miss sharing the responsibility. Sometimes.

When you're exhausted, below par or the children are 'playing up', the desire to escape is real. There have been a few moments when I have *seriously* wanted to do this, because I just haven't been able to see how I could keep going. 'I can't raise three children alone, like this.'

Except that I can.

Because I already am.

And you are no different.

We have so much strength, not only because of what we do for our child(ren), but also in how we manage to maintain a relationship with our ex-partner, after the love has diminished, in order to continue raising our children together. This contact with one another can initially be painful and make the healing process feel so much longer.

Having to accept that our former partner will still be in our life after separation, and that we will never have the opportunity to sever all ties – because we have the greatest tie of all – is a realization of its own. But we can make our peace with it and it's so much better for us when we do (see Learning 81).

Learning to share our children and assist them in constantly transitioning between parents and houses also has its challenges. Sometimes it just doesn't feel okay being away from them, and *that's* okay. I remember this well. Shortly after my ex-husband and I separated, I went away for a long weekend and left the children with him. I spent the whole weekend trying to control from afar, frustrated that he wasn't doing everything I had asked him to do. 'They're *my* kids!' I said. 'Except, they're *also* his,' my friend reminded me.

When you first separate, it's really natural to feel possessive about your child(ren) and to try and control the other parent – especially if you were wronged or didn't want the relationship to end. But no one owns another human being and, as long as there's no safeguarding reason why your ex-partner shouldn't spend time with them, you want your child(ren) to have a relationship with both of you. Make that your intention.

When the tricky days hit, we must keep moving and believing in ourselves and our paths as parents, which have so far led us to this point. Don't let your imagination drift off into the next 15 years – an overwhelming proposition for anyone – we'll get there when we get there, as we always do.

Rather, let's be as conscious as we can, actually be present in the moments we share with our children and trust in the good times that are coming our way.

While always remembering that *everything* we do comes from love.

I see your strength.

And you *can* do this.

(Because you already are.)

Learning 75

I AM ABLE TO ASK
FOR WHAT I NEED

'Ask for what you want and be prepared to get it.'

MAYA ANGELOU

S o much of a dysfunctional relationship is spent waiting for your partner to read your mind and figure out what it is you need. You could ask. But instead, you wait.

It's almost the final test of *how* 'good' (or bad) the relationship is. How well do they *really* know you?

I waited for so many things. For my ex-husband to give me the emotional support I thought I needed. For him to put the bins out. For him to remember how I took my tea.

These things mattered to me a great deal, at the time.

Yet, I could have just asked him, each time.

Now that there is only me to do what needs to be done, I find myself able to ask when I need some help (see Learning 22). If I don't ask, I'm not being a martyr. I'm managing; I can do it, and happily so.

It isn't a mind game or a test.

And this has also worked in an unexpected way, too. Not only can I now ask for what I need, I'm also able to verbalize what I *don't* need or *can't* do, without being concerned about causing offence. Once I would have said yes to *everything* and *everyone*, from a desire to please.

This is one of the greatest returns of empowering yourself and relying only on yourself.

Letting your autonomy guide you.

PART 7

AWAKENING

LIVING YOUR LIFE IN
A CONSCIOUS WAY

There hopefully comes a time in separation when we become comfortable with our new status.

We have motivated ourselves. We have asked the questions. We have listened to the answers and followed the signs. We have learned more about who we are than ever before.

We have woken up.

And we bask in the light of this wonderful enlightenment because now we *know*.

These next 13 learnings share the ways in which I have personally awoken and the ways in which this influences how I live my life today.

Learning 76
I AM NOT A CONSISTENT BEING

*'I mean how do you know what you're going to
do till you do it? The answer is, you don't.'*

J.D. Salinger, *The Catcher in the Rye*

After reading this book, you would be forgiven for thinking that I am now a consistent human being who has life sorted and always lives by my mantras and learnings. Yet during the editing of this book alone, I have been reminded how much I need to continue to prompt myself to live in awareness. We all do.

I've repeatedly heard that spiritual leaders who spend their entire lives immersing themselves in finding alignment and meaning do, too. I find this very encouraging. We're always learning and to be human is to be inconsistent and uncertain.

The goal is *not* to be a consistent being, except in alignment with oneself.

Growing up, I earned the 'affectionate' nickname Whimmy at home, because I never stuck at anything. I tried everything: ballet, tap, horse-riding, amateur dramatics, painting, piano, dog-training. Emotionally, I was fiery; I still can be. As an adult, I have frustrated others (and partners, especially) because I have changed my mind too often for their liking. I've tried and abandoned yoga, several times. I've almost been to Zumba. There are lots of domain names bought that never saw the glory of an actual website. And I've nearly upholstered a chair. The list goes on.

Other people's reactions made me believe that changing my mind was a bad thing. I have spent far too much time wishing I was different: 'consistent and stable, above all else!'

Now? I believe the exact opposite. I mostly thrive on uncertainty and on not always knowing what I'm going to do. I have had some successes from 'just having a go' and I have learned a lot about myself from being what society would call 'an emotional person' (I prefer 'open'). Feeling is the very nature of being alive. We would be robots, otherwise.

But I am still able to cause myself suffering whenever I tap into this social pre-conditioning – when I resist *myself*. Because the state of being a human that behaves consistently in action and emotion is a learned behaviour; it's one we are taught as we grow up and it takes time to undo. From an early age, we are conditioned to stick at things, work hard at them and control our emotions. Yes, it benefits us to have emotional awareness, but we must still be allowed to *feel*, change and grow. It is essential for our 'thrival'.

Some days, I have to really *try* to feel myself into a place of self-love and acceptance; to ditch my ego and listen to my soul.

Meditation has helped me with this. The idea of meditating used to scare the life out of me; any time I had tried it, I just couldn't shut my thoughts down. Then I heard Bradley Cooper talking about how he meditates for 20 minutes a day. Aside from the fact that Bradley Cooper could probably convince me to do *anything*, it made me think of meditation as an ordinary practice – like going for a run or any other beneficial habit we have. Because, when you break it down, meditation is nothing more than sitting quietly and being still. *Anyone* can do that.

The first time I tried to meditate again, then, I put on a piece of relaxing music and sat for what turned out to be 17 minutes – it felt like two. When I had finished, I felt unburdened and available; a vessel able to receive, not resist. It allowed me to love the soul I am and silence the ego I'm not.

Finally, after more than 40 years on this planet, I'm accepting that I'm not a consistent being, nor do I need to be. Separation has been one of *my* most important experiences in allowing this. On a very literal level, I married someone and, later, I changed my mind. Everything that has followed since has let me see that this is okay. Nothing bad has happened. On every other level, it has opened me up. Truly opened me up. It has taken me through a million emotions, made me doubt myself and empowered me. All at once.

And now I am able to *love* the fact that I am *not* consistent and enjoy wherever this might take me.

Because, it has led me here.

To a place where I *am* whole.

And I am free.

Learning 77

I DON'T ALWAYS HAVE TO UNDERSTAND

'Quiet the mind and the soul will speak.'

MA JAYA SATI BHAGAVATI

Once separation allows you to begin to live your life in awareness, you can find yourself seeking meaning and understanding in all you encounter, because it is thrilling knowing yourself and watching the pieces come together.

Sometimes, a moment of clarity is so great you want to shout it from the rooftops. At other times, you *know* you're on the brink of some imminent self-discovery but it feels foggy and out of focus; you see only distorted pixels and can't zoom out to see the whole picture.

These moments can feel as though you're going backwards because you're slightly in limbo. How did it all feel so clear and now, suddenly, it doesn't?

But: we are not meant to understand everything that happens, *especially* in the moment that it is happening.

So I try to exist in the awareness that I can never force the learning. It will come when it comes and, in the meantime, I will lean back from the fog in my head. Because trying to decipher it never brings clarity, only confusion and anxiety.

What I *do* choose to understand is the unfaltering presence of trust and gratitude. And I know that if I practise both even while I am feeling confused, the clarity – when it comes – will be another opportunity to reinforce their unparalleled role in all that I do.

It is *never* for me to question the process and I don't always have to understand it. And I know, very soon, I'll be desperately wanting to shout from the rooftops, once more.

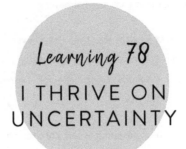

Learning 78
I THRIVE ON UNCERTAINTY

'Certainty is no good for us.'
BRENÉ BROWN, SUPER SOUL PODCAST

I am continually reminded that uncertainty – the unknown – is not the scary place we sometimes envision. It's a place of illumination. A place that allows us to discover desires, strengths and abilities we didn't even realize we had.

Brené Brown first introduced me to the actual concept of uncertainty. I had experienced it, of course, but only as a negative. Uncertainty used to make me feel uncomfortable and lost. I always wanted to *know*. But the very nature of being human is to be uncertain, and when we accept that, that uneasiness suddenly falls away.

Why would we fight against ourselves? What can that possibly produce but conflict and our own suffering? That makes no sense at all.

Separation helped blow the pursuit of certainty completely out of the water because it evaporated everything that I had told myself was true. Certainty – to control and to know what was next – was no longer an option. And anyway, how well had striving for it served me so far?

Accepting that we are unsure and vulnerable – and that we were created that way – is the start of learning to thrive on uncertainty. Because, once we have listened to what our vulnerability is telling us, and once we stop making a beeline for certainty, we are opening ourselves up to actually *live*. We aren't forcing. We aren't looking to *know* all of the time. Instead, we're saying, 'I don't know what's going to happen and that feels exciting.'

That feels like *being alive*.

When others are constructing plans around me, as the world loves to do, I choose *not knowing*. I trust that I will always feel myself into the place I want to be; and that, sometimes, I won't know what that place is until merely minutes before.

Then, later, I'll reflect and think, *Well, of course I was supposed to be there*. And yet, I could so easily have missed it, if I had allowed myself to get caught up in other long-standing plans I hadn't ever really wanted to make. I still make plans, of course; we all have to be in certain places at particular times. But I don't make plans for the sake of them or in an attempt to control every one of life's outcomes. I leave time where there is *nothing* planned so I am free to go where I feel I'm being called.

Uncertainty isn't for everyone – although it can be, with a simple shift in perspective – and those of us who thrive on it will likely frustrate the hell out of others for whom we are, in their eyes, the very epitome of disorganized, chaotic, indecisive or impulsive.

There is no right or wrong. Only what feels good to *you*.

Sometimes, when I fall back into habitual thinking, not having plans can panic me – especially socially or during times such as school holidays, for example. But when I'm in alignment I have such self-assurance that, even when everyone around me is planning, not only does it not bother me that my diary isn't full, it actively encourages me to keep living freely.

Stepping away is the dare.

And we've already done that, in separation.

It's time to enjoy the thrill of the ride.

Learning 79

I ALWAYS ALLOW MYSELF TIME TO TRANSITION

'When the wind of change blows, some people build walls, others build windmills.'

CHINESE PROVERB

Change is not something that all of us relish. It is a natural tendency to view change from a place of loss and fear: the *loss* of what we know and the *fear* of what is to come. This could be the very definition of separation.

We lean back into the fear when we should lean into the *transition*.

Transition allows us to embrace change with grace, patience and peace. We afford ourselves time to acclimatize, while using all of our past experiences to have faith that we *will*. When we're ready. As we always do.

Before separation, being a parent coerced me into learning about transition and embracing change. I used to swing between wishing time away and desperately wanting it to stand still, but there is nothing that keeps on changing as fast as a baby, toddler, preschooler, child, tween, teenager and young adult. If we don't keep up, transition and change alongside them, we find ourselves constantly mourning and idealizing the past, while trying to resist the swift passing of time.

Yet, it is this very natural passing of time that is the key to unlocking the door of transition, if we allow it.

When my first child started school, for example, my vibration was anxious, resistant and static; I didn't want this change. When my youngest started school, my vibration was content, forgiving, and flowing; I still had some natural anxieties about the adjustment that came with a suddenly empty nest, but the thing that made the difference was that I was allowing myself the time to transition – however long this took (only a couple of weeks, as it turned out, *because* I was kind to myself).

We cannot rush the process of transition – or the process of separation – as uncomfortable as it may sometimes feel. We have to simply trust in its transformational power (see Learning 46).

Transition is a crucial, gradual experience in which we create and grow *together*, alongside circumstances, people and the universe.

It is collaborative, not solitary (you're never alone).

It is continual creation over static existence.

And, once we master it and how to align ourselves during it, change is something we will no longer approach with great fear. Only great faith.

Learning 80

I AM NOT DEFINED
BY ACHIEVEMENT

*'Nothing feeds the centre so much as creative work,
even humble kinds like cooking and sewing.'*
ANNE MORROW LINDBERGH, *GIFT FROM THE SEA*

Most of us like to be good at something. For many of us, success in our work, relationships and everyday lives will become a huge defining marker of who we are.

I always imagined I would be successful, and 'achieve' in a career, and find 'true love' of the unattainable movie variety.

Well, I know how the latter worked out (so far) and – despite a traditional, good academic record – I never found my groove career-wise. Until my separation, that is, which coincided with my self-publication of *The New Mum's Notebook* and subsequent book deal. I think this is why I have the confidence and faith to follow my instincts – not to follow the crowd – when it comes to my own children's education. There is so much more to it than good grades.

So, in my adult life, I have been blessed because I have never been particularly defined by achievement; I had spent so long living without it.

All that abruptly changed when my ex-husband and I separated, and it reopened a whole world of possibilities for me. Suddenly 'true love' – which I have since redefined anyway – was back on the table. And I felt that sense of achievement when people told me how I was inspiring them because I was raising our three children mostly single-handed.

At the same time, I started to receive praise from customers, retailers and health professionals for *The New Mum's Notebook*, which was proving to be a steady seller. In the process, I became very involved in social media.

Gradually, I noticed that I was coming to rely upon this praise and validation. I started to believe what people said about me on social media – most of whom didn't even know me. My self-esteem became wrapped up in their opinions, much as your self-esteem does when you're in a relationship that isn't good for you.

I felt successful and valued when I was being validated, and less so when I wasn't. It's a common affliction, especially where social media is concerned; studies show that people experience a release of dopamine when they get likes, shares and comments.

I'd been managing to rebuild my low self-esteem after my separation and yet here I was, endangering it again. It made me realize that there was no way this could be a sustainable or desirable mode of living, and

I stepped back to consider the alternatives. After all, achievement is such a subjective thing and, if it relies upon anyone but *you* to validate it, it's also very fickle. You might be the shining star today, but next week it will be someone else's turn.

Stepping back gave me more time to do *real* things: such as cook a meal from raw ingredients for my family; tackle the washing pile and *actually* put it away; change the furniture around in my bedroom. And I noticed that I got *exactly* the same amount of pleasure (dopamine) from these activities as I did from social media and more success-orientated tasks.

This taught me that it isn't the nature of the achievement that matters but the *feeling* we get afterwards – the gratification is what we crave and become addicted to seeking over and over again.

And that can be replicated in a million ways, most of which have no association with how capable, intelligent, wealthy, loved, popular or successful we are (although those things can obviously give us joy and fulfilment, too).

After all, *anyone* can put away the washing.

Learning 81

I AM GRATEFUL FOR MY EX-PARTNER

'Because I always have a choice, I choose love.'

DEEPAK CHOPRA

My friend maintains that my ex-husband is my greatest teacher. He has been – and continues to be – the catalyst of my enlightenment.

I have learned so much about myself *through* him, our marriage and, most of all, our separation.

As our separation has progressed towards divorce, I have felt almost every emotion about and towards him: relief; indifference; empowerment; anger; sadness; jealousy; resentment; regret; compassion; understanding; acceptance. I have revisited these at various points over the past four years. I know I will continue to do so in our future.

These emotions are not dissimilar to the stages of grief because, of course, we experience grief through any sense of loss, not just through bereavement.

When I first wrote this chapter, my ex-husband and I were emotionally in the best place we had been in years and certainly in our separation. We could finally see each other's position, or so I thought. I was feeling optimistic about the future. We had had a rare moment together, when we had both admitted to each other our roles in our relationship's demise. I was choosing to see his strengths, rather than dwelling on his weaknesses. If we had managed to do any of this in our marriage, we might have managed to make it work. But so many of us need time and space to truly grow, and find that we do that better alone. Couples also need to grow together and at a similar rate – and we were most definitely not doing *that*.

A couple of weeks later, we were back in a place of conflict and miscommunication again. It hit me hard, perhaps harder than anything else that has happened in recent years. Because, despite the growth steps I felt we had made, I saw the reality of how far apart we actually still remained. How far apart we might *always* remain. I had fallen into the trap of expecting from him again, of hoping and of placing *my* security in his ability to act from a place of love towards me.

I *know* that I never need *his* loving self to be *my* loving self.

But I had forgotten, temporarily.

And this was my prompt: to remember that I must try to remain in a loving state, even while others around me do not. There are some days when it's a tall order, but it can be done as long as we remain aware of our emotions and our inclination to react. In the meantime, it is perfectly acceptable to establish boundaries – such as temporarily blocking all communication – while emotions (on both sides) settle.

So, the universe continues to show me my path; to show me that I will have tricky times ahead to navigate, as we co-parent our three children – as any parents do, together or not. It also continues to show me that I must lean back and react without conflict or I'll be building momentum in the wrong direction.

I *must* choose love if I don't want to lose my way. Or my mind. I *must* choose to love him (yes, I did just say 'love').

Because, in doing so, I will continue to grow as *my* true, open and loving self; every human being's sole purpose. Whatever my ex-husband does. Whatever *your* ex-partner does. They're only catalysts in helping us to fulfil this purpose (which can, I do acknowledge, sometimes be a great personal challenge).

We can either choose to find them frustrating or be grateful to them for the insight.

The latter will hurt us far less.

Learning 82
I WILL KEEP DOING THINGS DIFFERENTLY

'If you do what you've always done, you'll
get what you've always gotten.'

TONY ROBBINS

Having the courage to continue changing and to tread new paths you haven't yet cleared takes practice, even though you're already living the biggest change, in separation.

We have to keep aligning ourselves and making ourselves 'dare' to do things differently if we are to keep growing.

I have enough life experience to know how most situations in my life will habitually end up, before I've even engaged with them.

For example, whenever I've accepted an invitation out of obligation or politeness (or the fact it's six months away and is just an abstract date as far as I'm concerned), the chances are I've ended up cancelling nearer the time, because to go would cause me to fall out of alignment with myself, and that never feels good.

Don't accept it in the first place, then.

For years I have dipped in and out of curious sobriety. When I haven't wanted to drink, but have put myself in a social position where the opportunity was there and everyone else was drinking, I would usually find myself doing what I've always done and joining them – probably overindulging, too.

Don't go unless you're confident enough to stand tall in your own intentions.

After such scenarios, I would wonder why I had been so frightened of choosing the path I hadn't yet walked; the one that led somewhere I didn't know, often on my own, away from everyone else.

Maybe because sometimes we just fall out of awareness and into old habits. We find ourselves still following old patterns of thought and letting ourselves be influenced by what others think, making the story up in our heads again (see Learning 28).

We have to keep aligning ourselves with ourselves.

Now I do things differently and I will continue to do so, plunging myself into the unknown, when it feels good, without fear of pushing myself – and often others – out of the comfort zone of *knowing* in the process. Because we *know* that certainty is no good for us (see Learning 78).

When I manage to do this, I feel aligned because I am staying true to *myself*. And there is always some new and wonderful discovery awaiting me. To take just one example, on the subject of sobriety: as I write this, I haven't touched a drink for three months. Unlike on any previous occasion when I've dabbled with sobriety, this time I have trodden new paths, doing things sober that I once thought were always enhanced when accompanied by a drink. A warm summer evening. Parties with friends. A festival. Holidays. Meals out. Doing these things differently and fulfilling *my* intentions has been liberating and infectious.

What *else* can I do in a new way?

This might mean we make choices and decisions that others don't understand or desire. But that's okay. We are all different in our intentions and each of us has every right to act from a place of self-intent where we acknowledge what's important to *us*.

Because there isn't *anything* that is worth you accidentally following someone else's agenda.

And forgetting your own.

Learning 83

I DO NOT NEED TO SHARE MY 'HARDSHIPS'

'Hardships often prepare ordinary people
for an extraordinary destiny.'

THE CHRONICLES OF NARNIA:
THE VOYAGE OF THE DAWN TREADER (FEATURE FILM)

Everyone is going through something. We don't necessarily realize this when we're young, unless we have a particularly empathetic nature.

As we age, however, we are exposed to more experiences, our own and others'. Some are good, some are not so good and some are heartbreaking. We become aware of the fragility of life and the common variances in personal circumstances; we understand that we are not the only ones with 'hardships'.

We are going through something, but so is someone else.

We won't always know they are, though.

While there are people who tell *everyone* what's going on in their lives because they need the sympathy of others, there are others going through something equally difficult – or even more so – who deal with it so silently that you'd never know anything was wrong.

I was once that person who liked the sympathy of others. I admit that sometimes I thought I was the *only* one having a difficult time. And I allowed it to consume me.

Separation changed that for me, forever. Sympathy was suddenly the last thing I needed or wanted. And when others learned about my separation, five months later, they said they couldn't believe I had been going through that and conducting myself so gracefully. If that was true, it was probably the first time I had ever dealt with *any* situation with grace and discretion.

It wasn't a false representation because my separation wasn't a hardship, as others possibly imagined it to be. The previous few years *had* felt false, while I'd been hanging in limbo, knowing the relationship needed to end but not knowing *how* it would happen.

Separation was empowering. It took me away from my natural tendency to be a victim or martyr. It transformed my inclination ever again to play either of those roles; faced with an uncertain situation, I think most of us would choose to operate from a place of strength, hope and faith – in ourselves.

So now, when I experience difficult times, I try to be gracious during them. I don't need to share my hardships with the general public (a few confidantes will suffice) or for others to know in order for my challenges to be valid. We're *all* managing circumstances and juggling lives and we just need to be there to support one another with a shared kind word, knowing look or smile.

Because we are all going through something.

Learning 84
I ASK MYSELF THE QUESTIONS

*'Once you get the questions right,
the answers always come.'*
JAMES REDFIELD, *THE CELESTINE PROPHECY*

Even when we live in a more enlightened, aligned state, there are times when we will still feel confused, overwhelmed, put upon, misunderstood or simply in need of more information in order to move forwards.

On such occasions, it doesn't feel right to deal with these emotions quietly. So we need to stop and ask ourselves the questions.

We must ensure, however, that we are asking the *right* question by sitting back and examining the one we *think* we want to ask, bearing in mind that often our questions – about another person's conduct, for example – are *really* about our own plight (see Learning 31). Dig deep and identify what's triggering the emotion, doubt or vulnerability you're currently feeling. Whenever I do this, my attachment to the issue and emotional response dissipates and I reach the *right* question. Then the answer comes.

I find that I am no longer scared of asking myself the difficult and uncomfortable questions now. Of asking myself something I might have once preferred to suppress. Of asking another person to be honest with me, about me or my conduct, if I need their insight.

It's how we unravel the truth when the truth isn't immediately easy to see and we can't move forwards without it.

And next time, we might be able to ask *fewer* questions because we have more experience at our fingertips.

We have more answers, because once we asked.

Learning 85

I ACCEPT THAT
THERE IS NO 'RIGHT'

*'Somewhere between right and wrong,
there is a garden. I will meet you there.'*

RUMI

When I first drafted the contents of this book, this learning was called 'I accept that some things may never feel right'. Because, at that point, it felt as though some things never would and my healing could only be found in accepting that.

For the first two years after our separation, I couldn't get past the reality that I would never again be with the father of my children. As I continued to make my peace with so many other things, I couldn't align myself with *that*. That would never feel right, I decided, even though I now suspect that that definition of 'right' was dictated by my society and environment, rather than by anything else. That was my particular mental block about separation; yours may possibly be different (or not).

Then, one day, I felt differently. It wasn't a conscious acceptance; just that when I thought about it, it no longer sat uncomfortably with me or caused a resistant vibration. It didn't feel right. It didn't feel wrong. *It just was.*

In that moment, I saw my growth – no doubt a result of every combined learning here. I saw that the perception of the word 'right' is as unique as each of us, so much so that it only ever has context in reference to ourselves. *What is right for me?* I saw that while some things – like my situation – might never seem *right* to others, to me those things could feel as good as I chose for them to feel.

There is no right or wrong. Only what feels good to me.

And this is such an uncomplicated way of living – without constantly analysing whether what you're doing/saying/feeling is 'right' or 'wrong', but instead seeking that which feels *good*.

We can *always* align ourselves by listening to our own feelings, rather than conforming to an ideology that no longer represents us and in whose values of *right* we had no say.

So actually, yes, 'I accept that some things may *never* feel right.'

Because they were only ever meant to feel good.

Learning 86
I CHOOSE MY INTENTIONS

'What is the why beneath your why?'
GARY ZUKAV, SUPER SOUL PODCAST

Have you ever realized that behind *everything* you do is an intention? An intention that you choose, whether you give it any conscious consideration or not. Intention is different to decision; it's the catalyst that informs what we choose to do.

Often, we aren't really clear what our *true* intention is and so we effectively send out a confused message into the universe. Gary Zukav talks about 'choice of intention' in his book, *The Seat of the Soul*. For him it is a fundamental creative act, so when we become an *aware* creator, we become more able to harness our creative capacity in a loving way. We can choose to create from a place of fear (which will almost always produce destructive consequences), or we can create from a place of love.

So we must ask ourselves *why* we want something – a partner; more money; a bigger house (see Learning 72). Where does your *why* come from? Fear or love? To take the example of a partner: do you want a partner because everyone else has one and you don't want to be alone (fear), or because you're so happy in yourself that you want to share this in building a loving life with another (love)?

Whenever I have acted in fear, from anger or jealousy or some other pain, it has resulted in me hurting myself, if not also others. It creates lack, inadequacy, and a feeling of being intrinsically flawed. It is never a pleasant experience.

When I *choose* to start from a place of love – and this takes awareness and practice – what follows often surprises me, simply because it is so wonderful I don't even feel that I've had to *work* for it (because, of course, I haven't). Just by redirecting my energy, I have allowed it to happen, with ease.

Our choice of intention *always* influences what happens next. If we aren't aware what it really is, how can we expect to get where we really want to go?

Always ask yourself, what is the *why* beneath your why?

Learning 87

I AM
INSPIRED BY OTHERS

*'If I can learn to understand this language without
words, I can learn to understand the world.'*
PAULO COELHO, *THE ALCHEMIST*

Undoubtedly, it is always our own alignment we must focus on. We are unique and we must not be distracted by comparing ourselves with others. That doesn't mean that we walk our paths alone, though.

The people that flow in and out of our lives are little markers – our guiding stars. They hold up messages – signs – we are to notice and receive. They are everywhere.

We know it as inspiration – that feeling of coming away from a conversation or an encounter lifted and knowing what it is we are to do next.

I feel endlessly inspired since my separation; since I became open again. Very infrequently do my encounters fail to show me something about myself. Because once we open ourselves up to this possibility – once we allow ourselves to receive these messages – the potential for learning and growth is all around us; not just in the 'big' lessons, but even in the mundane tasks we perform every day. Especially those, in fact.

Being inspired by someone else is nothing more complicated than being enabled by them, so that we can progress through our journey with a little more hope, joy and knowledge than we might otherwise have done without them.

So, I am inspired by the small messages and the way in which others walk their path. The school mum who's late but doesn't rush her kids and instead chooses to enjoy their walk together, as I so often don't. The person with mobility issues who reminds me that being able to go for a run is nothing but a privilege and a joy. The single parent whose 'hardships' are undetectable beneath their warm greeting and smile, when sometimes I just want to shout about my problems at the top of my voice.

These people inspire me to be more graceful and more allowing. To align myself, where there is still alignment to be made.

They keep me company, as I walk my own path.

They're my guiding stars.

And they are everywhere.

Learning 88

I GIVE MYSELF TO ME

'All that I am I give to you.'
Church of England wedding vows

Maybe it's no surprise that so many marriages end in separation and divorce, when we make such grand gestures to one another.

They are, of course, just words, but they are steeped in tradition and the concept of what we believe it means to be in a relationship, especially a marriage. These words create an image and we allow them to form at least some of our expectations, often when we are young and have next to no understanding of what a lifetime of being someone's partner will actually be like.

People who separate or divorce talk about feeling free again, eventually. Often, they say it is the best thing that has happened to them, because they have had a chance to rediscover themselves and question who they are – essentially what this book is all about.

After all, so far we've already explored living without conflict, gaining emotional awareness and managing ourselves financially and practically.

So I'm not sure we can, or would want to, revert to that traditional all-consuming form of relationship after such a liberating experience. That we could ever view another relationship as *giving ourselves* to another in the quest for self-fulfilment. That we would ever *need* to.

We find 'The One'. And it turns out to be ourselves, all along.

For me, at least, there is a part of me forever changed by my separation. The need to be someone's partner has been replaced by a desire to be, *if* I choose. But the idea of 'giving myself' entirely to another feels undesirable and completely unnecessary.

Instead, I have learned to give myself to *me* because that is where I am most comfortable. That is where I *must* be more comfortable. Enjoying my own space. Loving myself, unconditionally.

All that I am I give to *me*.

PART 8

NEW BEGINNINGS

MOVING FORWARDS
INTO YOUR FUTURE

Once we get closer to knowing ourselves better, we can begin the amazing journey of moving forwards into a meaningful future.

Everyone's future will look different, but the strides we all take in walking towards it can be just as strong and aware.

Here's where I've walked, so far, on the other side of separation; 23 glorious strides and learnings that have shaped *my* new beginning.

I hope your new beginning is just as glorious.

I absolutely know that it *can* be.

Learning 89

I TRUST THAT LIFE IS ALWAYS WORKING OUT

'Every experience I have is perfect for my growth.'
LOUISE HAY, *TRUST LIFE*

My friend has a wonderful phrase, which I have adopted and pretty much live my life by now: *life is always working out.*

She highlights this on the 'good' days. She especially reminds me of it on the days when I am finding it hard to stay in alignment with myself; when I might encounter self-doubt or disappointment.

Life is always working out.

And I have found it to be an incredibly powerful sentence that can instantly diffuse my emotions and bring me back to the moment in hand.

Because if I believe and accept that what is happening to me *right now* – no matter how undesirable it might feel – is going to propel me forwards in the direction I'm meant to be going, it is very difficult to resist it. It would actually be rather foolish. I'd be standing in my own way.

Resistance, as we've discussed, is the voluntary process that *creates* suffering in response to our pain.

Repeating this phrase to yourself and believing in its truth stops you fighting against the current and allows you to flow more easily downstream to what awaits you: the next moment that can't exist without this one.

Life is *always* working out.

Learning 90

I AM INVIGORATED BY MY FRIENDSHIPS

'Don't underestimate the power of friendship.
Those bonds are tight stitches that close up the
holes you might otherwise fall through.'

RICHELLE E. GOODRICH, *SMILE ANYWAY*

I am certain that one of the reasons I am so content being on my own is down to the wonderful friends and acquaintances who surround me.

In addition to the friends I already had, the universe has brought so many new friends into my life since separation. It's given me who and what I need at the exact time I've needed them. There are friends I have known for fewer than three years who have such a special place in my heart; with whom I am so aligned, through circumstance or outlook on life, that I can't imagine I might never have come across them.

I have chosen to invest more in my friendships since separation because I have had time and reason to do so. It's reminded me why we should *never* sideline friendship in favour of romantic relationships. Friends are the constants in life, if we allow them to be so, whether we ever have another healthy romantic relationship or not.

The right friends invigorate us and raise our vibrational energy. It is never too late to make new ones, either. Someone doesn't have to have been your best friend since you were 11 years old for there to be a strong allegiance *now*. Never pass up the opportunity to forge a bond with someone; you don't know who they might help *you* become. And vice versa.

If you're finding it difficult to do this, check your energy. Sometimes, very naturally during challenging times, the aura we project is closed and withdrawn. That attracts *no one* who is going to be good for you. Smile, relax your shoulders, unfold your arms, open your heart space and see what happens.

Remember what we talked about in Learning 22 and how connecting from a place of love is contagious and attracts more of the same. It works. It really does.

Because we all want to be around someone like that.

Someone like the true, loving you.

Learning 91

I AM EXCITED
BY MY FUTURE

*'It's the possibility of having a dream come
true that makes life interesting.'*
PAULO COELHO, *THE ALCHEMIST*

Possibility. Opportunity. Uncertainty.

These things – and more – excite me, because this is now what my future looks like. Or rather, I have absolutely *no idea* what my future looks like; and that is intoxicating.

Of course, the future can also look like this with a loving partner by our side but, for many of us, it doesn't or didn't. It felt predictable and as though we were going through the motions of a journey that was all mapped out.

We all have a degree of commitment. Work. Children, perhaps. Others who rely on us for their wellbeing – elderly parents, siblings, pets. Hopefully *not* a houseplant, if you're as horticulturally challenged as I seem to be.

But, outside of these, separation suddenly gives us just *us*. Only us to decide what we desire and how we want to live.

Sometimes, I allow myself to exist in this state of possibility and just notice it, without feeling compelled to do anything with it at that moment in time.

I can actually feel the energy of possibility flowing around my body. And, often, that is enough to raise my vibration and remind me of all that I *can* have.

It's a liberating way to be. And because the universe is on our side, there's no pressure to pursue it. Instead, we can trust that we'll never miss out on an opportunity.

We'll act when we're meant to. And we'll be ready.

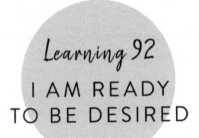

Learning 92

I AM READY
TO BE DESIRED

'When we delight in ourselves, we attract others to us.'

REGENA THOMASHAUER,
MAMA GENA'S SCHOOL OF WOMANLY ARTS

Sexual awakening starts with the moment we feel, 'I am ready to be desired', whether we fulfil this desire or not.

Sometimes, and certainly initially, just like it is with possibility and hope, our recognition of the feeling is enough.

Because reaching this place where your desire for yourself yields a yearning for the desire of another is an awakening all of its own, especially if it's been years since you felt this and you never expected to experience it ever again (see Learning 58).

Being psychologically open to feeling desired brings its own sense of coming alive again as you actually sense the energy of desire coursing around your body.

Acting on that desire physically is something else altogether. Don't rush to fulfil it or give it away. Let it begin with this.

The feeling.

Anticipation. Lust. Want.

And because like always attracts like, once you feel this sense of desire deeply and authentically, your energy will do the rest.

Wanting to be desired is about sharing this amazing energy and having it reciprocated. It's not about wanting validation or needing someone else to boost your self-esteem. If you let that be your motivation, desire usually has the opposite effect and lowers your self-esteem, because you will have a different type of energy coursing around your body. As a result, you'll make poor decisions, while expecting great, validating consequences: a one-night stand, for example, that if you're honest was perhaps never really casual in intention on your part.

You deserve to be desired for desire's own sake. Because you are desirable. Because it feels good and it makes you feel *alive*.

This stage is not about milestones or fast-tracking your way to the altar (see Learning 93). If you just want to enjoy and *be* enjoyed, go forth (safely).

Sexual awakening, post-separation, is pleasurable and intoxicating, when you're truly ready and you allow it to be.

So own your experience. Because desire always begins and ends with us.

Learning 93
I TAKE MY TIME ON MY TERMS

'I need not sell my soul to buy bliss. I have an inward treasure born with me, which can keep me alive if all extraneous delights should be withheld or offered only at a price I cannot afford to give.'

CHARLOTTE BRONTË, *JANE EYRE*

Starting a new relationship after separation is exciting and scary, all at once. 'Is this going to go anywhere?' 'Do I *want* it to go anywhere?' (Probably the most pertinent, nagging question of all.)

I met someone about a year after separating. It was a true universe moment in which I manifested him the morning of the day I met him. Everything that followed did so with ease. He was kind, passionate and, most importantly at that stage in my separation, *interested* in me. He changed my experience of relationships and my view of how someone else could see me.

As the months went on and the friendship started to encroach upon relationship territory, I found myself asking a lot of questions. On reflection, the questions mostly weren't even mine; they were seeds sown by others: 'What's going on?'; 'How's it going?'; 'What do you think will happen?'

I was just enjoying it; that felt good and enough.

So try to silence the voices in your head. And in other people's heads too. Because relationships after separation have their own set of rules. *Your* rules. You don't have to size this person up and think about whether you'll ever want to cohabit with them/marry them/reproduce with them/live happily ever after together. You've just done much of that with someone else. If you like someone and enjoy spending time with them, you can just go with that, for now. Or forever. Or until a different set of circumstances feels good.

Live in the moment. Savour the uncertainty. You deserve it.

New relationships can make you feel really self-conscious, especially if you were with your last partner for a long time and lots of people knew you together, as a couple. It can feel a little like being in a goldfish bowl: 'Is everyone watching?'

They probably aren't. (Some probably are.)

You might naturally be excited about this new person in your life but you don't really know what *you* think about them yet. So, in the early days, weeks and months, it is perfectly okay to establish your own timeline and terms; if children are involved, it's advisable.

It's easy, amidst the revitalizing power of meeting someone you like and find attractive, to get carried away on the wave of romance. You've maybe been without romance for some time and eventually fulfilling that longing for companionship and physical touch can be intense.

But be wary of declaring your undying love publicly or via social media. Wait until you're really, really, really sure. And then wait a bit longer.

Keep it private – keep it for you – until you've worked out what *you* want. Never share it at all, if you don't feel inclined.

Take *your* time.

New relationships post-separation, especially if you were married and/or had children, are less about hitting milestones, and much more about being with someone who allows your soaring soul to fly higher.

Far above the clouds.

For however long it lasts.

And wherever it goes.

Learning 94
I LISTEN TO MY HEART AND SOUL

'The mind creates the abyss and the heart crosses it.'

NISARGADATTA MAHARAJ

The first 'proper' relationship after separation is a pivotal one.

It may last. It may not.

Regardless of how it turns out, it's the relationship that will bring you back to life in so many ways. It's special and you'll remember it for this, always.

In the early days, it can feel heady and intense as you rediscover your sexuality and see yourself through someone else's eyes; someone who thinks you are sexy and incredible. This is a flattering endorsement (not that your self-esteem *needs* it).

In time, if the heat wears off and the steam clears, leaving you – or them – to see and feel things differently, that's okay. No one said this particular relationship had to be forever. You may love it for what it was. And you never have to rationalize its demise; so much in life is only ever meant to be experienced, not explained.

There is a tendency, after separation, to doubt your role in any relationship that follows and then ends. Maybe it *is* you who's the problem; you who can't make things work. Especially if this is implied by your new partner, practically echoing your ex beforehand. They can't *both* be wrong, can they?

And yet, it's never about who is 'right' and who is 'wrong'. Only about what feels right for *you*. A break-up is never one person's 'fault', even when it seems obvious, for example in the case of infidelity. *This* we already know. If we feel that we need to, we can do the work to understand how we got here, *this time*.

If there are things that bother you about your new partner, it is very likely that these are actually prompts for you to respond to something inside of you that you've yet to resolve. When things feel right, there is no effort to be made. Those bothersome niggles wouldn't even make it onto a pros and cons list because you'd never be writing one in the first place. You would just be comfortable, despite everything else.

Simply put, you can't make sense of a relationship until you have made sense of yourself and aligned yourself. So don't doubt yourself or wonder whether you're self-sabotaging (you're not). Don't allow yourself to be influenced by your new partner's desire or love for you. Don't allow yourself to be influenced by *anyone*.

If your instinct is that *this* relationship isn't right, it's a calling from your soul for you to continue finding *you*. Once you're stable in that place, the perfect person will be in your life and it won't even matter that they're there (lovely as it will be that they are). Because, as we said in Learning 24, when you are in perfect alignment with yourself, holding your vibration regardless of what *or who* happens around you, everything and everyone else becomes the wonderful icing and sprinkles on that amazing cake you already are.

Hearts rule here, not thoughts.

Listen to yours.

Learning 95

I ALLOW THINGS
TO HAPPEN AS THEY WILL

'Trust and allowing are the same thing.'

ABRAHAM HICKS

In Learning 29, I talked about forcing decisions and why we don't ever need to do this.

The more time that passes since my separation, the clearer this has become to me. If I don't know, I lean back, I wait and I allow. It is one of the biggest changes I have made in the way I now live life. I force very little and I am happy *not* knowing. I maintain that living in uncertainty is the greatest, most liberating and exciting gift that separation has given me. What will today bring me?

And I always figure it out. In the end.

Despite the fact I had played an active and willing role in our separation, on the day I received divorce papers from my ex-husband I felt sad. A bit angry. Slightly nostalgic. Regretful. And definitely rejected.

I sat on those papers for over three weeks, unable to contemplate them. Then, one day, I had a really nice and unexpected conversation on the phone with him. We put some things to bed and agreed to focus on moving on and raising our three children, apart but together.

A couple of days after that, we happened to be at a Halloween party together, with our kids. It was fun. Easy. Normal, even. Well, our *new* normal, anyway.

At the end of that week, feeling renewed courage for new beginnings, I rearranged my bedroom furniture and, without any pre-planning, I found myself looking at the divorce papers. Right there and then, I knew I was ready to sign them; to say goodbye to that part of my life and truly start the next one.

And I did.

That moment was a euphoric one. A milestone I never thought I'd see, least of all welcome. And it happened of its own accord, in its own time.

It was another reminder to me that all I ever have to do is allow things to happen, as they will, and trust that all will become clear.

Because it always does.

Learning 96
I TRUST IN MY SOUL'S ABILITY TO SOAR

'Your soul is that part of you that existed before you
were born and that will exist after you die.'

GARY ZUKAV, FROM SEAT OF THE SOUL INSTITUTE WEBSITE

The further I travel on this journey of separation, the easier I find
it to trust in my soul, the universe and the truth that *life is always
working out*.

I simply can't deny that it is or that, for me, this path has been
completely illuminated by separation. I truly believe that had my
separation not happened I would still be trying to find my way in
the dark.

I have more and more pleasurable experiences. I crash less often,
less hard; and I emerge quickly from the debris, with fewer or no
scratches. And, when I feel like I've learned all there is to learn, I'm
shown that my soul can soar even higher.

It doesn't matter if souls and universes aren't your language. You don't have to be a spiritual leader or devote yourself to three months of silence to be able to benefit from *really* getting to know yourself; your soul – that part of you that is more than just your body, mind, tissues and organs.

In his book *Spiritual Partnership: the Journey to Authentic Power*, Gary Zukav talks about authentic power and multi-sensory perception: the alignment of your personality with your soul and the ability to receive information *beyond* the five senses – sight, hearing, taste, touch and smell. Both draw you to matters of the soul. You may already have caught a glimpse of yours if you've started to want to live life more meaningfully or to want to share with others your gifts, which you were born to give.

My soul feels like an inner voice whispering an instinct in my ear, but it's stronger than that and it comes from (seemingly) nowhere. I feel it, I never think it. My friend says she saw my soul the day a complete stranger in the park asked me for change. He needed to use a payphone so he could call the council and resolve an issue with his accommodation; instinctively and without question I offered him the use of my mobile phone.

I think the soul is the part of us that is true, open and giving. The part of us that recognizes our own authentic value and worth and, in turn, always feels like sharing and helping others realize theirs, too. The part that realizes we are all the same in essence, so we never have cause to judge or compete.

Most of us will lose touch with our souls, at some point and often. Many of us will find our way back through our experiences, if we allow this to happen.

And those of us who are *really* willing to listen, will soar higher and higher.

The more we learn to fly.

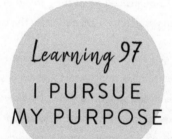

Learning 97
I PURSUE
MY PURPOSE

'The meaning of life is to find your gift.
The purpose of life is to give it away.'

PABLO PICASSO

It may take time to understand and feel your purpose – what you are here on this planet to *be* – but each of us has a purpose. It's okay if you have no idea what yours is yet; it can take time to discover and reveal it.

I use the word 'be' rather than 'do' because I think our 'doing' is multiple and variable; merely the actions we carry out in response to fulfilling that which our soul desires – *our purpose*. No one's purpose is to become a lawyer, for example, but it might be someone's purpose to help uncover injustice.

While we're all here ultimately to discover our true, open and loving selves, each of our souls also has a unique gift to bestow.

You may have always known your gift and stayed connected to it – amazing! – or you might still be putting together the pieces of the puzzle and learning as you go. I am definitely the latter.

Looking back, I can see that 'sharing experience' was my gift from a young age; being open and honest was (and still is) my natural inclination. I have always sought to understand myself and others and to look at *how* we survive: my university dissertation was on human isolation and the effects upon human behaviour, despite being a student of English literature rather than psychology.

Writing became the 'action' to fulfil my purpose. I wrote a small booklet about 'surviving university'. Upon leaving, I toyed with journalism, but I could never get a career off the ground; I didn't know why. Now I know that, while writing was the medium that set my heart alight, the route of traditional journalism and reporting didn't make my soul soar.

That was not *my* gift to bestow.

Years later, I shared my experiences of motherhood through a blog I called *Surviving Motherhood*, and I wrote two books that followed, very naturally and instinctively.

My being – *to share that which enables us to survive* – and my doing – *writing those experiences down* – were united in purpose. It took me until I was 37 years old to discover this.

Separation has shown me that my purpose remains strong. It's willed me to continue pursuing it through the very act of writing this book – a book I said I'd *never* want to write and share, when my friend predicted that I would.

But I have had an overwhelming desire to understand how I've 'survived' separation. And to share that with you.

Because I've found so much good in it.

I couldn't not give that gift away.

Learning 98

I LIVE MY LIFE
WITHOUT PURPOSE

'Do anything but let it produce joy.'
HENRY MILLER, *TROPIC OF CANCER*

We spend so much of our lives creating, proving and achieving with a goal in mind, we forget the pure joy of doing something without any purpose whatsoever.

Simply because we want to.

Simply for pleasure.

Simply for ourselves.

Separation has given me the luxury of the quiet time I was missing, to be able to spend time without purpose once more, like I used to as a child. Children are so instinctive about living their life without purpose, until we detach them from their inclination; far too soon and absolutely.

Spending time in your life without purpose is wonderful. It is freeing. It is a simple indulgence. It can be *yours*, with ease.

Do something for no other reason than it lifts your vibration. Because not everything you touch must lead somewhere, nor must it touch someone else, for it to have value. Paint a picture no one else will see. Play an instrument no one else will hear. Write a diary no one else will read. Have moments when it is about nothing but *that moment* and *you*.

And no end result.

Remove the goals. Remove the pressure. Remove the obligation.

Reclaim your instinct to live *without* purpose, some of the time. Because it is still there, inside of you.

You'll be amazed what truth you find, when you lose yourself in pleasure.

And you weren't even looking.

Learning 99
I VALUE
MY PRIVACY

*'Travel and tell no one, live a true love story
and tell no one, live happily and tell no
one, people ruin beautiful things.'*

KAHLIL GIBRAN

I n a world that has the ability to share *everything*, instantly, the lines surrounding privacy are less *blurred* and more *completely erased*.

In the search for truth and meaning, we must not confuse privacy with pretence or being false.

We can still be our honest, true and loving selves and *not* have to share everything, or even *anything*.

While I've shared very personal experiences of motherhood, anxiety/ post-natal depression and aspects of my separation, there is much I have kept back.

Not sharing every thought that enters my mind, every decision I've made, every mistake I've regretted or every relationship I've had, has for me been a great learning of separation. Indeed, it started with separation, when I chose *who* I wanted to share that with and *when* (see Learning 10).

I value that so much because, when we share, we naturally invite comment, opinion and, so often, judgement.

But some things are just for me.

And some things are just for you.

Preserve their beauty.

Learning 100
I LET OTHERS
TAKE CARE OF ME

'Individually, we are one drop.
Together we are an ocean.'

RYUNOSUKE SATORO

I t is not easy to allow others to take care of you when you've been looking after yourself for so long.

Separation is an empowering state for all the many reasons we've talked about here. You've grown in assertiveness and motivation. You've gained great insight into how wonderfully unique you are. You've learned how to express yourself in alignment with yourself. And you're proud of your independence and ability to cope and thrive. You might feel that you *never* want to give that up.

And you don't have to.

Letting others take care of you isn't *essential* – you don't *need* them to because you know you can take care of yourself. You are doing a wonderful job of that (I hope). Letting others take care of you is *nice*. I have loved the moments when I've had a cup of coffee brought to me, dinner cooked for me or some help making a decision.

We forget how nice that is when we're so used to flying solo. Allowing others to look out for you, to do things for you, to take on some responsibility, is like letting out a huge, deep breath that you didn't even realize you were holding in.

Being cared for gives you some respite from that. It makes you feel valued, as it does for those taking care of you.

You *are* doing a wonderful job, but it's also perfectly okay to let others in and let them help you in whichever way you or they desire.

You deserve to have that every now and again.

Everyone does.

Learning 101
I ALLOW FOR SOMEONE ELSE'S POINT OF VIEW

'It is difficult to express inner pain, and we all do it imperfectly. What may seem like anger and frustration from others is often the best they can do.'

DEEPAK CHOPRA, *THE DEEPER WOUND*

How many of us consider someone else's point of view before our own? Not many, I suspect.

It certainly doesn't come naturally to me, so it's something I am trying, very consciously, to do. I don't always manage it.

And I can absolutely admit to seeing my ex-husband mostly through *my* point of view, *my* experiences and *my* inclinations.

This pretty much amounts to me misunderstanding him. Often. I'm sure he doesn't always understand me either.

Allowing for someone else's point of view is not the same as trying to ascertain what that point of view is. Unless they wish to share it with us, we can't possibly have any idea; we can only speculate.

It's simply acknowledging that they *have* a point of view and that it can be different to ours. Because our experiences, inclinations and interpretation of those are probably not the same.

Why does this help when you're going through a separation? Because it reduces conflict. It stops you thinking yours is the only point of view that's valid. It stops you making the story up in your head (see Learning 28). And it allows you to remain in a state of compassion from which you can view your ex-partner not from a place of anger, resentment or disappointment, but from one of love, which ultimately secures *your* peace.

We all handle ourselves differently and how *you* deal with a difficult situation is not necessarily how someone else will.

Allow their point of view.

Allow *them*.

Learning 102
I SEE THINGS IN ALL THEIR GLORIOUS COLOURS

'Your thoughts, words and deeds are
painting the world around you.'

JEWEL DIAMOND TAYLOR

In my new, bright future, there is no right and there is no wrong. There is no black and there is no white. There is only a spectrum of colours so vast and so open to interpretation that it is impossible to define them all.

And who would wish to?

Amidst these colours lies every unique experience we've ever had: every thought, every opinion, every happiness and every sadness.

Our very own rainbow.

This colourful spectrum represents open-mindedness. For if there is no right or wrong, what else remains but to be open and receptive, without judgement?

No scenario needs to be understood to the point of resolution. It is already resolving itself right now, with or without our loving input and whether or not we believe this.

And no scenario will resolve itself in the same way, no matter how similar the circumstances may seem. The person whose partner has been unfaithful, for example, will not meet the same resolution as someone else whose partner has been unfaithful.

There is no right and there is no wrong.

There are so many colourful and intricate layers that we will simply miss if we choose to apply a textbook answer or a tried and tested approach to everything we encounter.

Separation has been *my* rainbow for, just as a rainbow reflects, refracts and disperses light, so too does the state of separation.

And it has helped me see *all* the glorious colours around me.

There is so much understanding and acceptance to be found in the merging of these palettes. There is also so much love.

Connect with *your* rainbow.

I COMPROMISE WITHOUT SELF-SACRIFICE

*'When you say "yes" to others make sure
you are not saying "no" to yourself.'*

PAULO COELHO

S hould we ever *really* compromise?

Yes and no.

Yes, if the compromise does not mean taking ourselves out of alignment. No, if the compromise actually results in self-sacrifice.

Any role that we perceive to be sacrificial – mother, carer, worker, partner – creates feelings of burden and resentment. This is because once we perceive that we have *given up* something, we must seek to make our effort worthwhile. To compensate. And who can possibly thrive in any relationship that swings on such a paralysing and inevitably disappointing pendulum of responsibility and guilt? Neither the giver *nor* the receiver.

Whenever I've compromised with my ex-husband *against* my own instincts and desires – out of alignment – it has ended in conflict. Because I have given inauthentically, and that has created expectation within me to compensate for my *sacrifice*. When he hasn't responded with whatever expectation I was hoping he would demonstrate – gratitude, reciprocation, acknowledgement – I have been angry with myself *and* him. Slowly I am learning not to do this and learning that it is essential to factor myself in, because creating boundaries is healthy.

In this way, separation teaches us *how* to compromise, as we learn to put ourselves first; not in an obstructive way, but in a way that sees us looking out for *ourselves* at the same time as looking out for someone else. We then compromise in a way that feels *comfortable* and authentic. My friend, who has a very healthy relationship with her husband, says she has never *really* bent without a little self-intent – by which she means that she doesn't really compromise unless she's comfortable that it's to her advantage too. I think women, in particular, often bend without *any* consideration for themselves.

Compromising in alignment with your own desires, as well as someone else's, is the only way *to* compromise. Only then can it bring peace. For you. And also for them.

Otherwise, we must call it what it *actually* is.

Sacrifice.

Learning 104

I WILL KEEP LEARNING THE LESSON

'Some things cannot be taught;
they must be experienced.'
ROY T. BENNETT, *THE LIGHT IN THE HEART*

There is a habitual part of ourselves that doesn't *really* believe we keep on learning.

Sometimes we think we *know*, because we have reached a point of insight, enlightenment or pure joy in which momentarily we have it all figured out. Then the universe taps us on the shoulder and says, 'Hang on, I've still got more to show you.'

The lesson that follows is often uncomfortable, painful and surprising, because *we thought we were there*. How disappointing to discover that we aren't.

That's how it was on the occasion I mentioned in Learning 52, when my ex-husband's conduct towards me – because it came directly after the most open conversation we had had in years – was all the more painful for me.

I was more disappointed in *him* than ever. I was disappointed in *me* because I had allowed myself to hope. I was disappointed in *us* because we were still so far from being on the same page. But to make separation truly successful there is work to be done on both sides, and we can't rely on the other person to engage with that process in order to be able to consider our own efforts successful.

So, I should never have expected him to behave in a certain way, or been looking for *my* alignment in *him*. That desire for respect, compassion and grace can only ever originate from within me. Only me. Always me.

That was the lesson that day. Again. And it is up to me either to *know* it or to keep doing the work and keep learning it.

Either way, we have a responsibility to ourselves to be aware and to understand that separation – and life in general – is not about reaching a conclusion whereby everything makes sense and we are comfortable in certainty. It's about being open enough to admit that we *don't* know everything, being willing to learn in good time and trusting in the ultimate lesson, even when we have no idea what it is going to be.

Because, whether we believe it or not, we are *always* learning.

I REFLECT ON
THE HAPPY TIMES

*'Because it is not lasting, let us not fall
into the cynic's trap and call it an illusion.
Duration is not a test of true or false.'*
ANNE MORROW LINDBERGH, *GIFT FROM THE SEA*

We have all experienced times in our relationships where we were happy. Blissfully so. Those times still exist, even when the partnership ceases to.

We can still think of them fondly. Every single moment. They do not have to become tarred with the ending of this particular love story.

In that moment, it *happened*. You were there. Your ex-partner was there. Together. That moment cannot unhappen.

We are a culture obsessed with permanency. We want every individual moment of joy to last forever. Every moment of pure love to last forever.

But no moment can.

And possibly it is our very inability to accept this that leads us to move from relationship to relationship in the pursuit of endless joy and love.

Four years on, I allow myself to reflect on the happy times I shared with my ex-husband. Not with regret, sadness or 'what if', but with love, amusement or amazement, depending upon the memory in my mind. Sometimes, I share them with my children; they enjoy hearing about when we were happy. It's good for them to know that we once were, together.

Because we had a lot of happy times that I do not wish (or need) to erase. And when I remember these times, it enables me to find that place of love from which to view him.

He gave me something, once. I gave him something, once.

And *those* moments of pure joy and love will exist forever.

Because they cannot unhappen.

And I would not want them to.

Learning 106

I MAKE THE MOST
OF NEW OPPORTUNITIES

*'Everything is either an opportunity to grow or an
obstacle to keep you from growing. You get to choose.'*

WAYNE DYER

W e've established that separation *is* opportunity.

It is renewal. Renewal of the way you live your life. Renewal of
what your future looks like. Renewal of *you*.

As we move beyond the early, self-discovery stages into awareness
and living our lives in a more conscious, aligned way, we are able to see
that opportunity lies within *us*.

Because not only do I make the most of new opportunities that arise,
sometimes I create them.

An example of this was when I decided to get a dog. I was out
running one day when I passed a golden retriever. I've always loved

golden retrievers and had a crossbreed growing up. I experienced a connection with that golden retriever and, by the time I got home, I knew we were getting one. By the end of that same evening, I had arranged to go and see a litter at the weekend, 90 miles away. The puppies were ready to leave on Friday; I was going on Saturday. It all fell into place with complete ease.

There were, of course, many reasons *not* to get a dog, if I had chosen to focus on them. All I could see, however, was the new opportunity in front of me. When others warned me about how much I'd need to change my life, what a commitment having a dog was, and how much work they were – 'worse than having a newborn!' – I couldn't hear the words. (Indeed, we frequently offer the same warnings to mums-to-be: no wonder so many start motherhood from a place of fear.)

By contrast, I had no fear; the prospect of change and another opportunity to grow – for my kids also to grow – brought excitement. I knew that this dog was coming for a reason because it was all happening so quickly and instinctively. So I put my faith in that. Intuition overrides analysis; there are now studies that actually prove this.

In a very gracious way, it no longer mattered to me what others thought. I could see their reasoning and even understand it, but I couldn't *feel* it. They weren't *my* reasons or *my* experience.

It didn't work out with the puppy. After two months, it became apparent to me that the dynamic was chaotic for all of us, including the dog. Waiting in the wings was a friend who had always believed that work commitments would prevent him from ever having a dog of his own, but who chose to take this puppy on. Their connection was *strong* and he found a way to make it work because of that. I felt no shame or guilt for giving the puppy up. Rather, I chose to see myself as the facilitator of their relationship – my role all along.

And that confidence has come purely as a result of being separated. Of knowing *me* better. Of knowing my capabilities better. Of knowing that *life is always working out*, whatever the outcome.

So there is *only* opportunity ahead of me now.

And I want to keep allowing every single one.

Learning 107

I FIND A WAY TO CELEBRATE THE 'FIRSTS'

> 'Just when the caterpillar thought the world
> was over, it became a butterfly.'
>
> PROVERB

The first year of separation is full of milestones you probably won't want to celebrate. The first time you go away without your partner. One another's birthdays. Other people's birthdays. Family holidays, whether it be Christmas, Hanukkah, Eid, or *any* significant time in your calendar that prompts you to reminisce and think about where you were 'this time last year'. (More about creating new memories in the next learning.)

But what about focusing on those *other* firsts, instead?

The first time you *manage* to go away without your partner. The first time you figure out how to dispose of *that* Christmas tree. Celebrating your birthday in a *new* way and actually in a way that *you* choose. My 40th birthday was the best I've ever had because I knew it was only down to me to organize it and so I did. It was exactly how *I* wanted it to be; I didn't spend it expecting someone else to come up with the goods and then feeling disappointed when they didn't (because they never *could* read minds).

There is a *lot* to celebrate, once you really start looking. Every day offers cause to celebrate *yourself* in some way, because those firsts just keep on coming – no matter how huge or how insignificant they may seem – and you keep on acing them.

And if the *only* thing you can find to 'celebrate' is the fact you've survived a difficult 'first' day, such as an anniversary, then mark that and notice your strength and determination to go forwards, from a place of love.

Failing that, remember the best thing about firsts: they only happen *once*. And I think they *do* get easier. Or you just learn to handle them, because, like everything, you get better with a little practice.

And you know that you're going to come out the other side, into a brighter light, once more.

Because you always do.

Learning 108

I CREATE NEW MEMORIES
AND TRADITIONS

'Newness hath an evanescent beauty.'

HEINRICH HEINE

Post-separation, we have to learn to redefine all of the memorable dates, annual holidays and social events with which the calendar seems to torment us.

We have to view these from the perspective of our new situation.

We have to learn to create new memories and new traditions.

We cannot live in the past and what was.

My first Christmas as a separated woman and mother actually wasn't that difficult because I spent it with my ex-husband, so although we weren't living together as a married couple, little had changed in terms of how we celebrated Christmas as a family.

The following year was a different story. My ex-husband took the children for Boxing Day with his new partner, and while I did have plans at home, it became such a strange day for me that I ended up spending it alone, in a sort of paralysis. I was so relieved when it was over.

That year taught me that I could not have a 'normal' Christmas without my children. I would need to make *new* traditions going forwards, whether that involved travel, dinner with friends or a trip to town. The new tradition was almost irrelevant; it only mattered that it wasn't what I *used* to do – dinner at home. The absence of my children was too great.

You may feel something similar, regardless of whether you have children or not; the absence of your *partner* is too great.

The third Christmas, however, came and went with ease. My children went to their dad's on Boxing Day for three days. I didn't miss them because we had had a lovely Christmas Day together and they were happy. Instead, I enjoyed the time that followed, for me.

Establishing *new* traditions is important. I introduced some to reframe Christmas for us all, retain the magic and give my children something to remember when they're older. I decorated their bedrooms with lights and baubles while they were at school and nursery. I made Christmas Eve boxes. We put the tree up together and decorated it.

On Mother's Day, I ignored all the flowers, breakfasts-in-bed, lunches out and pampering – all the clichés social media and commercialism told me I *should* be receiving at the hands of my children's father because my children were too young to do it all themselves. Instead, I dropped some flowers and a card round to my own mum and then I spent the day on the sofa, watching films with my kids and ordering a 'dirty' pizza. I think it was our best Mother's Day yet.

We have to learn to create new memories and new traditions.

We cannot live in the past and what was.

New traditions give you an opportunity to revisit old traditions, ones that you hadn't even realized might no longer serve you well. And you'll be much more flexible about growing and developing *with* traditions in future, not enduring *despite* them. There is no attachment; if they don't suit this time, you'll find a new one that does.

Remember how easy it is to romanticize what was and how good the mind is at creating thoughts and false realities based on what it desires in that very moment (see Learning 30).

Don't help it along by indulging these thoughts, because this is never going to be helpful. Always give yourself the best possible chance and distract yourself (put away that washing!). Never recreate the same scenario. Do something different. Make it about *something else*.

It doesn't matter what it is. As long as it isn't sitting around drinking wine while listening to sad love songs on the radio. Don't do *that*.

Because what I can absolutely promise you is that experimenting with new traditions, which may or may not stick, is one of the most liberating and invigorating benefits of separation.

The future is suddenly an adventure.

And the memories you'll be creating will be spectacular.

Learning 109
I AM ALWAYS CO-CREATING IN THIS LIFE

'There's no such thing as being alone in the universe, and so there's no such thing as creating alone. Everything...is a co-creation.'

GARY ZUKAV, SUPER SOUL PODCAST

I have come to realize that we do nothing *alone*, even when we perceive we *are* alone.

There is no creation in isolation. We are enveloped in a patchwork quilt of our experiences, influences, environment, energies, vibrations and connections. We are always co-creating in this life.

When I wrote *The New Mum's Notebook*, I said afterwards that I felt as though it had written itself. I still feel this. My friend agreed: how could I have written it on my own, without the universe's guidance and input, when I was going through a marriage break-up at the time?

And there have been parts of *this* book that I haven't even *known* or understood until the point at which I sat down to write them. I started chronologically and then swiftly went out of order, writing whichever Learning from the contents page I was drawn to that day. There were so many times when I found that the chapter I had randomly chosen to write related perfectly to the ones written before and after it.

Then there was the day I changed my bedroom around (see Learning 71). I hadn't intended to remove the symmetry but that's exactly what happened. And I cannot forget the kitten my children waited six weeks for, who then went AWOL – along with her breeder – on the day we were due to collect her. Several hours later, we collected a completely different kitten, already named Cosmo (yes, really), who is so perfectly matched to our family that we must have been destined for one another all along. All these were co-creations with the universe. Because there are *no* coincidences or accidents.

So I accept the wonder of my patchwork quilt. I will never question any of those patchwork squares that comprise my circumstances, relationships, work and daily activities. Instead, I will be grateful for my quilt's comfort and trust in its weight.

For I do nothing alone.

Learning 110
I BELIEVE I CAN
(AND I WILL)

'This is your story. Let it unfold.'

SHERYL SANDBERG

Growing up, I remember having this sensation of *knowing* – a sensation that I didn't really understand.

I believe.

As I got older, I sporadically lost touch with it, usually when things weren't working out as I'd hoped or planned (and therein lay my misconception, because now I know that *life is always working out*, whatever the outcome).

I can't remember the exact moment I secured for my self-belief the level of permanence that I mostly have today. I know that it happened, very gradually, after my separation. A situation I had been led to believe was undesirable became for me quite the opposite; if I could believe *I can* through that, surely I could believe *I can* through anything.

I can.

One moment along that journey was an evening with two friends, when we did a mood board about how we wanted our lives to look (a mood board that manifested several pretty amazing things for me). Another moment was when a friend took me under her wing and showed me what can happen when you just choose to believe and allow (thank you, Sarah).

There is the knowingness that has come from every experience, challenge and pleasure I've lived since my marriage ended.

And that is pretty much how I live now. In belief. Every single day. I *choose* to believe. *Always.* In everything around me. In myself. In my abilities and authenticity. In my connections with family, friends, acquaintances and strangers. In my circumstances. Even when things feel stuck or uncomfortable, I have decided that I will just believe in *all* of it.

I will.

Any of us *can.* And we absolutely deserve to believe in our own abilities and authenticity. Because when we do, not only can we create anything we desire, we also create self-belief in others, as our vibration radiates and helps them choose to believe in themselves, perhaps for the first time.

What greater gift can we bestow than that? From personal experience as a recipient, I can tell you: there is none.

So silence the questions.

Choose to believe.

Because *whatever* comes your way, *believe* you can and you *will*.

Look where it's taken you, so far.

Where will you go next?

Learning 111
I CHOOSE
THIS LIFE, TODAY, AS IT IS

*'Whatever the present moment contains, accept it as if
you had chosen it. Always work with it, not against it....
This will miraculously transform your whole life.'*

ECKHART TOLLE, *THE POWER OF NOW*

The final lesson in my separation journey – so far – is succumbing to the wonderful simplicity and purity of acceptance.

I give myself to *today*. I pledge to notice *today*. I choose *today*, however it presents itself, and wherever and in whatever state I find myself.

No conditions. No exceptions. No bargaining.

Today, as it is.

Whether it is soul-soaring or uncomfortable; flowing with ease or swimming upstream; purposeful or stuck.

Because to date every single experience in my life – especially all those I have had since my separation – has shown me that I am meant to be *here*. My story is *this one*, and every chapter has been written by me. Whether I realized it or not at the time, I certainly realize it now.

And I have complete faith in me – in who I am today, what I 'write' next and who I am to continue becoming.

I no longer wish I were different. I no longer wish I had made alternative decisions. I no longer wish my life looked any different to how it looks like *right now*.

The best stories never let you see what's coming next. They keep you guessing and wondering. The ending is a complete surprise. Except in our story, however, we know there is no ending.

So keep wondering in *your* story. Because to wonder is *not to know* and that uncertainty is what will keep you putting pen to paper, what will keep you feeling *alive* and what will remind you that you are *always* the author.

Keep writing it. Living it. Loving it.

And allowing your soul to soar.

I'll see you, way up above those clouds.

And beyond.

ACKNOWLEDGEMENTS

To Michelle, Jo and everyone at Hay House for believing so instinctively in this book and giving it the wings to soar its way into the universe. Thank you! I have not stopped pinching myself since that December day I stepped into your offices and we had our amazing meeting.

To my editors, Emily, Julie and Stephanie, for editing this book with such warmth, intuition and encouragement, and for helping to produce such a beautiful cover. You understood this book so easily.

To my agent, Julia, for being my vibrational match. It is so much fun working with you and your belief in me always spurs me on.

To my dear friend, Sarah, who 'manifested' me, even though I didn't know what you were talking about back then. You said I would write this book in your kitchen in Brockley, when I turned up on your doorstep one day in tears. I remember thinking, *I'll never want to write about this*. So many of your words from our WhatsApp conversations have made their way into this book. I'm sure you'll recognize them. Thank you for being my spiritual partner, helping me soar and live my life in alignment. You are wonderful.

To brave and graceful Donna and Claudia, just two of the friends that separation has gifted me. You have shown me that there are *no* circumstances in which a person cannot soar. You should be proud of yourselves every single day.

To all the thought-leaders who serve to make the world more loving, and who help me on my journey every day. Especially Oprah, for introducing me to so many through her Super Soul podcast, which accompanies me on many a joyful run.

To my parents and my sister, I live the life I have so confidently because you are always there in the wings. Thank you for always supporting us.

To my ex-husband, for our three beautiful children and for all the learnings in co-parenting. We don't always get it right, but we keep on going.

To my children, Eva, Ivy and Joseph, thank you for embracing a decision you didn't make with love, encouragement and vigour. I am endlessly inspired by who each of you are.

And, finally, to you, navigating separation and lost love. I hope this book helps you on your unique journey, back home to *you*.

There's no place sweeter.

Much love

Amy x

FURTHER RESOURCES

Amy's blog

Surviving Motherhood (www.amyransom.com)

Books

Anne Morrow Lindbergh, *Gift from the Sea* (Chatto & Windus, 2015)

Brené Brown, *Daring Greatly* (Penguin Life, 2015)

Dalai Lama and Desmond Tutu, *The Book of Joy* (Hutchinson, 2016)

Deepak Chopra, *The Deeper Wound* (Rider, 2016)

Eckhart Tolle, *The Power of Now* (Hodder & Stoughton, 2001)

Esther and Jerry Hicks, *The Law of Attraction* (Hay House, 2016)

Gary Zukav, *Spiritual Partnership* (Rider, 2010)

Haruki Murakami, *What I Talk About When I Talk About Running* (Vintage, 2009)

James Wallman, *Time and How to Spend It* (W.H. Allen, 2019)

Marianne Williamson, *A Return to Love* (Harper Thorsons, 2015)

Paulo Coelho, *The Alchemist* (HarperCollins,1995)

Podcasts

Unlocking Us, Brené Brown

Oprah's Super Soul Conversations

The Hay House World Summit

ABOUT THE AUTHOR

Kate Darkins Photography

Amy Ransom is an author and a solo mum of three children. Her writing career didn't begin until the age of 36, when she started a blog called Surviving Motherhood in which she shared stories and insights about life with her two- and four-year-old children. She went on to self-publish *The New Mum's Notebook* – a sanity-saving journal to support new mums.

In 2016, Amy separated from her husband after nine years of marriage and three small children. She maintains that separation has been her most positive experience yet.

Amy has always been interested in the universe, alternative thinking and attracting her own outcomes. She believes that our journey, while always our own, is most enlightening when we travel it together, and that we all deserve the support and reassurance to enable us to travel it with joy. This is the ethos behind everything she writes, and this book especially.

Amy has appeared on numerous radio and TV shows, including Radio 2's Steve Wright in the Afternoon, Radio 4's Woman's Hour, *This Morning*, BBC News, Sky News and Channel 5.

 @amyransomwrites

 @amyransomwrites

 survivingmotherhooduk

www.amyransom.com

HAY HOUSE
Look within

Join the conversation about latest products,
events, exclusive offers and more.

f   Hay House

🐦   @HayHouseUK

📷   @hayhouseuk

❤️   healyourlife.com

We'd love to hear from you!